THE

BITCOIN

BOOK

THE BITCOIN BOOK

A Beginner's Guide to the
Future of Finance

MATTHEW UNDERHILL

DISCLAIMER

Great care has been taken to make sure the information presented herein is accurate, however, some opinions expressed are solely that of the author. The information in this book is for educational purposes only and is not intended as personal, financial or investment advice. The author does, however, advise that the reader should never invest and trade money they cannot afford to lose. Should the reader wish to buy or trade cryptocurrencies, they should first consult with an independent professional financial advisor. The author cannot be held responsible for financial losses incurred, whether government currency or cryptocurrency, through any information, practices, products, or services that are mentioned or recommended within this book. None of the digital assets referenced in this book are publicly endorsed by the author in any way, nor is their inclusion in this book a recommendation to buy, as they are included for educational purposes only.

Dedicated to

Louise, Elizabeth, my family,
R.P.K, Prometheus, and Satoshi.

In a country well governed, poverty is something to be ashamed of.

In a country badly governed, wealth is something to be ashamed of.

- Confucius

CONTENTS

Disclaimer..v

Acknowledgements......................................xv

Introduction..xvii

PART I

WELCOME TO THE NEW ECONOMY

A Brief History Of Money....................................1

The Big Difference Between Money And Currency 7

We Are All Satoshi 19

Bitcoin Is Open Source 29

Dispelling A Few Myths 31

Enter Bitcoin: A New Money For The People 33

What Does A Bitcoin Look Like? 41

Where Can We Use Them? 43

Why Are They Worth So Much? 47

Why Is The Price Of Bitcoin Expected To Rise? 51

What Will A Bitcoin Be Worth In The Future? 55

It's Too Late To Buy Any Bitcoin 61

The Bitcoin Standard 65

PART II

THE TECHIE SCIENCE BIT

Cryptography 77

Blockchain 81

Keys 89

Bitcoin Address 93

Bitcoin Wallets 97

How Are Bitcoin Made? 107

Consensus 117

Confirmations 119

The Lightning Network 125

What is a Fork? 129

PART III

THE NEW ECONOMY AWAITS YOU

Alternative Coins 131

What Is Bitcoin Cash (BCH)? 139

Some Negative Opinions 147

Is Bitcoin Mining Bad For The Environment? 155

How Adoption Might Grow 159

Crypto Exchanges 163

The Different Types Of Digital Assets 171

Top Coins Explained 177

What is An ICO? 185

Introducing the STO 189

Crypto Security 191

Facebook's Libra 205

Global Adoption And Development 209

Ways To Acquire Bitcoin 217

What Kind Of Bitcoiner Will You Become 219

Bitcoin Investing/Trading 223

Global Emergencies 229

Closing Thoughts 233

Further Education 241

Appendix A: Lingo, Slang And Acronyms 247

Appendix B: Buying Bitcoin On Kraken 255

Appendix C: Hardware Wallet Security 271

About The Author 275

Index 277

ACKNOWLEDGEMENTS

I would like to thank all my family and friends who have supported me while I wrote this book. Moving homes twice, IVF, the birth of my daughter, my second cancer diagnosis, subsequent operation and the writing of this book have made these last two and a half years stressful and rewarding in equal measure. My Wife, Brother, Dad, C.J, Justin, Steven and my illustrator The Black Shuck, were extremely helpful and without their input, I would have never finished this book.

INTRODUCTION

◆◇◆

Welcome to Bitcoin! The future of money has finally landed! Bitcoin is a new technology and currently a highly volatile speculative commodity. It is the world's first borderless, censorship-resistant, immutable, programmable, and cryptographically secured hard money. But what does all that mean? Hopefully, this will all be answered in the coming pages. You will learn lots about this new technology in this book and hopefully, it will give you the confidence to buy some should you wish to do so. Bitcoin is an extremely vast and confusing subject. It covers multiple scientific disciplines that frankly most people would struggle to fully understand, let alone master. But just because it is technical, it doesn't have to exclude people from learning the basics. I hope that the information I have detailed here can be read by all people and that it will give them a better understanding than the media may have.

Why have I written this book? Bitcoin is now in the public eye, and adoption is starting to rise. However, many people still do not understand what it is, what makes it so special, where they can buy them, how to store them or why it has gained so much value in these last few years. I hope to answer these questions and to show people why it was invented, how it works, and detail why this new technology *could* change the world for generations to come.

Why should you learn about Bitcoin? The genie is out of the bottle now, and the technology cannot be uninvented. It, or something very much like it, will be mainstream in the next few years and anyone who doesn't understand the basics or know how to use it will be left behind. Imagine what it would be like for yourself or someone you know, who couldn't use the internet or something so simple as a smartphone or a tablet. Cryptocurrency is here to stay, and it *will* impact our lives over the coming decades. If the technology itself is not your primary interest and you are more focused on the price then that is fine. Yes, it is true that many people in the West are here for the price speculation, and that the price has increased significantly. It's price also fluctuates dramatically; however, these large percentage swings are expected to stabilise over the coming years as this new economy matures. Interest in Bitcoin increases as it's price rises. It is human nature I guess to follow the herd, especially when everyone is talking about it. Bitcoin's price has risen massively from its inception when each one cost only fractions of a penny, and as we will see many people believe it will rise to unimaginable amounts over the coming decade. If your interest in Bitcoin is solely a speculative financial one, now is the time to learn some of the basics before you dip your toes in. To save repeating myself at the end of each chapter, I would like to state that the reader should research every aspect of Bitcoin that they either have an interest in or wish to pursue. Take the process of making bitcoin for example (known as mining) which we discuss later in the book. It would be advisable for the reader to learn more about it after reading my short chapter on the subject and not rush out immediately to buy mining equipment. This process of additional learning should extend to all facets of Bitcoin, especially the subjects of regulation and taxation. Simply put I have tried my best to detail many of the processes and functions of Bitcoin, but it would only be prudent for the reader to do additional research before they jump into Bitcoin headfirst.

So, who am I? I am just your average blue-collar worker. I am not a technologist or computer scientist, and most certainly not a Bitcoin expert. I am not particularly computer minded, and definitely not a computer geek. I work an average job, in an average industry. So, what am I above average in, I hear you ask? Well, that's why we are here today because I have lots of experience explaining Bitcoin to beginners!

I am not a financial advisor but do find the subject of investing and financial independence interesting. I am the earliest adopter of Bitcoin that I know, having been in the space since early 2015. I have seen the downfall of Bitcoin proclaimed by countless commentators, to now see many of them change their tune and some even praise and adopt this new technology!

I have also helped a handful of family and friends enter the space and hope that this book will assist others wishing to join the cryptocurrency revolution. While I'm not working or learning about this new economy, I can be found on long walks with my family, tinkering with our campervan, clay pigeon shooting and playing rugby. I live in the South West of England with my lovely wife and daughter, along with our two dogs.

We live in uncertain times, already in 2020 we have seen the coronavirus pandemic cause panic around the globe and even whispers of an overdue economic crash can now be heard. How will Bitcoin fair in these times of turmoil? Is Bitcoin uncorrelated to the traditional markets? Is it a safe haven asset like gold that can be relied on in times of instability? These questions can be posed more than answered, as Bitcoin is still relatively young, and these two recent threats have only just surfaced. Either way, we will look at some of these points in this book and see what Bitcoin can potentially offer the world in times of need. In the coming chapters, we will learn things like, what Bitcoin is and what it isn't. We will learn how old it is, why it was made, along with how it works. You will soon realise that the subject is very vast and at times a very technical beast. However, I hope to arm you with all the necessary information to make the subject easy and hopefully enjoyable to learn. Bitcoin is a new technology, it is so new that few people know how it works, or what its benefits are!

Most people who have heard of Bitcoin know that it is a new type of internet money, but the understanding stops there. We will see that Bitcoin is very different from our current monetary system, for example, it enables people to bank independently between themselves for the first time in history! This is one of its main features, but it has many more. So, sit back and prepare yourself for your beginner's guide to the future of finance.

THE

BITCOIN

BOOK

PART I

WELCOME TO THE NEW ECONOMY

A BRIEF HISTORY OF MONEY

Firstly, and before our hike across the green pastures of Bitcoin gets underway, I feel we should take a brief look back in time to see where we have come from, financially speaking. For some clarity and as a reference point, we will look at the history of money and then we can shift our focus onto the difference between money and currency. This information will be quite important in understanding why Bitcoin is so special and groundbreaking. Money is such an integral part of our lives but like so many things, such as our health, it is something we take for granted. Maybe not the actual labour of earning it or the ownership itself, but more the concept of money. It was here long before we were born, our parents and grandparents didn't tell us of a better money long past, or that we should be wary of bankers, so we generally accept the status quo. Nobody teaches us anything different, so we except that money has always been the way it is, and therefore it must be the absolute best it can be, otherwise, surely somebody would have changed it at some point over all these years, right?

For thousands of years and only up until the early 1900s money had real value! Old money, the type used by our great grandparents, is referred to as sound money. This is money that holds its value. Is today's money not valuable?

Well yes, but only just. It is definitely not valuable like money once was. Old money used to be much more valuable. In the coming pages, we will delve into this subject and uncover why our modern money is pretty worthless in comparison and is becoming less valuable year after year.

Originally, many moons ago, people used the bartering system to trade and transact with each other, "how many carrots do you want for that chicken"? (as my dad would joke). Carrying pockets of carrots around to trade with or piggybacking your pig around on the off chance you wanted to trade during the day became tiresome for most folk, so things had to change. Slowly over time and in small pockets around the globe, people started to trade with locally scarce items. These items ranged from all manner of objects from certain seashells, glass beads, large carved limestone discs,[1] to rare feathers and even whale's teeth. Tulip bulbs have even been used as money! That is right in the 1600s in Europe, there was what later became known as the tulip bubble. Where tulip bulbs were used as money, with some bulbs reaching sums of thousands of pounds each. It did not last too long, and the tulip bubble is likened by some Bitcoin naysayers as being one and the same thing.

---

[1] These circular discs ranged in size with some being nearly 4 metres in diameter. They are called Rai stones and were used as a form of money on the Island of Yap around a thousand years ago. I share a link to learn about them later and you will be surprised how these stones share similarities with Bitcoin.

Eventually, all these items were replaced with precious metals. Enter silver and gold! To begin with, these were rough nuggets or even small shavings and flakes. If the individual was extremely wealthy, the metals were sometimes fashioned into long strips that the owner coiled around their forearm. Over time the use of these small nuggets evolved into the properly minted silver and gold coins that we are familiar with today. For thousands of years, silver and gold coins became the recognised money that gentlemen and kings would use to trade. The size, weight and emperor or monarch's face on the coin might have changed, but these metals were, and still are today, globally recognised as commodities that have value. Why?

- There is an associated cost in acquiring these materials. Both a financial cost as well as a labour-intensive cost. That is before you spend even more time and energy refining it and then minting it into a usable coin. Throughout history, most monies have shared the same qualities, that among other points, they are rare and costly to source and manufacture. Logic would suggest that because it has taken time and money to produce the coin, it should hold some degree of value.

- Relatively speaking, gold is in short supply. As we will learn later, many commodities or items that are scarce also have a high value, especially if they are sort after. From the trading cards or collectable toys we had as children, to antiques and classic sports cars, if an item is rare and is also desired by many people it will warrant a high price tag.

Old money had value! Gold has ticked all the above boxes for thousands of years and it still does to this very day. As a side note, that's why SAS soldiers and RAF pilots have carried gold sovereigns on missions behind enemy lines. Because everyone knows what a gold coin is and depending on the situation, a single coin could buy you food and water, or munitions, safe passage or even provide you shelter or protection.[2] At the time of writing, one gold sovereign coin costs around £360. A little over a hundred years ago, a gold sovereign cost a single pound! (20 silver shillings in old money). People would like to tell you the price of gold has gone up significantly since then, and that is why there is such a difference between the 1900 and 2020 price. The true cost of gold may have increased moderately over the decades, through increased investment demand, but a *major* reason the same coin that once cost £1 now costs £360 is that our money has been devalued over this time frame. Remember that inflation (additional money printing) causes currency devaluation. This means that the real cost of everyday items such as cheese and butter or even houses goes up. Through the excessive printing of our banknotes, the purchasing power (or value) of our government money has gone down, so it now costs more money to buy the same item. As we know gold is rare, and because many people want to own gold, its value is strong and can rise over time. The opposite can be said for government money, it is cheap to produce and is far from rare. If there is an abundance of a commodity its value lowers and lowers, just as we saw in 2020 with the global oil price. During the first couple of months of the pandemic, the need for oil plummeted so much that the futures price of oil dropped below zero! As we move to the next chapter, we shall learn more about the overproduction and subsequent devaluation of our government money and see that it has been happening for many years.

---

[2] For your reference, the British gold sovereign coin was first minted by Henry VII in 1489. Modern sovereigns have been continually minted since 1871 and weigh 7.98 grams, roughly 1/4 of a Troy ounce (31.1 grams). They have a gold purity of 91.6% (22 carats).

THE BIG DIFFERENCE BETWEEN
MONEY AND CURRENCY

Can you see where this is going yet? At times this chapter may be a little painful to read, however, it will be required learning for many people. Here we will learn the sorry history of how we have ended up in the financial state we are now in, and ultimately why Bitcoin was invented.

Once upon a time, a US dollar and a British pound were redeemable for gold. This was called the Gold Standard. Over the centuries it had become tiresome and risky to carry gold and silver around and it was also tricky to transact with, so the bankers designed the first banknotes. These were effectively paper IOU's or promissory notes, that allowed you to carry your gold around in paper form. Fast forward to the late 1800s and the UK, USA and much of the world was well established on the Gold Standard. This ultimately meant that for every paper pound/dollar in existence, there was an ounce of gold in the bank's vault and that the holder of the paper note could swap it for the gold whenever they wished. Gold, a real commodity with lots of history as being real money! Since the middle of the 1900s, the American dollar has become the most widely used currency on earth as most of the trade between countries is conducted using US dollars.[3] For this reason, it is known as the global reserve currency. The fact that the dollar was backed by gold gave people around the world assurance that it was money worth holding and trading with.

For various reasons such as decreases in the global gold supply and increasing populations, two costly world wars and all the associated rebuilding worldwide that was needed, it became less

---

[3] Virtually all the world's oil is also purchased using the dollar, and in these cases the US dollar is nicknamed the petrodollar.

feasible to use a commodity like gold to back the US dollar, at least this is what we are told. There may be other reasons, but they are too conspiratorial to mention here at this time. Ultimately, the death of gold-backed money started in the early 1900s. Which incidentally coincided with the creation of the American central bank, the Federal Reserve. Britain had been on a Silver Standard for hundreds of years and migrated to the Gold Standard, courtesy in part, to Sir Isaac Newton who was the Master of the Royal Mint. Britain came off the Gold Standard in 1914, which allowed the government to print extra money for the war effort, via our central bank, the Bank of England. Winston Churchill then put Britain back on the Gold Standard in 1925 before leaving again in 1933 (likely in anticipation of the looming Second World War).

America started to leave the standard the following year and in what later became known as the 'Nixon shock' the world fully exited the Gold Standard in August 1971, when President Nixon took the US dollar *completely* off the standard and terminated the Bretton Woods agreement which had been in place since 1944. Many people believe money (be that British, European, or American) is still backed by gold. This is not true. It once was, but now it's just worthless paper money. It is in some ways no different to the paper money used in the famous board game Monopoly. The main distinction is that government money is made, supported, and protected by our governments. While Monopoly money is printed by the game manufacturer Hasbro. Some people would argue there is little to distinguish the two types of paper money. From this point forward, the dollar, the world's reserve money, turned into being a simple currency and arguably lost all intrinsic value. The pound is also now not money, but just a simple currency also known as legal tender.

What is our currency backed by then? Well, that would be nothing. Well nothing of any real value anyway, just the decree (an order that has the force of law) that our governments will do their best to uphold, support and maintain it, via controlling its supply and adjusting its interest rate. For this reason, our coins and notes are officially called *fiat currency*, after the Latin decree fiat, meaning 'It shall be' or 'Let it be done'. To make this point clear and from now on in this book, we shall no longer refer to pounds, euros, and dollars as money.

It may seem petty, but as it is not accurate to call them money we shall call all 'government money' exactly what it is, fiat currency, currency or even just fiat. It may be hard referring to it this way, as we have all spent years calling government currency…money. However, there is a big distinction to be made, and now that you are learning what sound money is, what gold and silver have offered the world for centuries and what Bitcoin is striving to accomplish, we shall use the correct terms wherever possible.

When the world came off the Gold Standard, it allowed America, Britain, and Europe to print extra currency *without* the need for the extra gold to back it. Other governments around the world followed suit. This almost endless flow of free currency flying out of the printing presses has been used differently over the years by each subsequent government in office. Some have built and modernised with it, while others have used it to stave off recessions. One worryingly consistent use has been to fund the almost endless stream of wars that we have seen in recent history. The First and Second World Wars, The Cold War, The Korean War, Vietnam, Falklands, interventions (covert and overt throughout all of Africa and South America), along with the recent wave of wars throughout much of the middle east. *All* possible in part, because our politicians abandoned the Gold Standard and made it legal for themselves to create currency (and debt) out of worthless paper! To see the list of wars from 1945-1989 follow this link https://en.wikipedia.org/wiki/List_of_wars:_1945%E2%80%9931989 and you will be shocked at how there have been over 200 wars and conflicts over this relatively short timeframe.

You should be embarrassed to see the British and American flags associated with many of these. One can only imagine how much death and misery have been caused in such a great number of hostilities (and how much debt has been created to fund them with all the munitions, troops, tanks, ships, and jets required). The military-industrial complex that both Presidents Roosevelt and JFK warned us of, seems to have done very well under the fiat currency system! Remember that many of these wars may not have been financially viable if we remained on the Gold Standard. Using fiat currency has allowed Western foreign policy to forcefully and brutally dominate much of the world since 1944.

Many people also believe that the rampant currency printing, known as QE (quantitative easing) that started after the Great Recession in 2008 is propping up the world's stock markets and holding off the inevitable crash that some believe *should* happen. By printing additional currency, they are making the situation worse, whereas many feel a painful jolt to the system (with companies failing, and the associated redundancies etc.) would *almost* be preferable to the more damaging situation that additional printing could bring. Mainly hyperinflation! Where the value of your *entire* currency system devalues massively, resulting in the images we have seen in places like the former Weimar Republic (Germany), Zimbabwe and more recently Venezuela, where wads of currency were needed to buy cheap items such as a loaf of bread or a gallon of fuel.

With unchecked currency printing many tycoons, bankers, and big businesses grease their own pockets with this newly created currency, as it is handed to them first. Their associates, politicians, family and friends can also benefit from this newly created currency before it loses its value and trickles down to the common folk below, known as the Cantillon Effect. The concept of printing your currency with no regard for the future implications is similar in some ways to how a young adult issued with a credit card for the first time...overspends. This ability to buy what you want, when you want, with seemingly 'free' currency seems magical, and the notion of paying it back is a distant half thought that can be worried about another day. Right now, there are holidays, new televisions and fancy clothes that must be bought. Or in the case of governments, there are faster and more powerful submarines and aircraft carriers. So long as the monthly repayments can be covered, let's not worry about the underlying debt. Having a currency no longer tied to gold reserves, also allowed for a new technique within banking to exist. It is called fractional reserve banking. This allows banks to create additional currency out of thin air, directly from our deposits. I will let you research this function of modern banking for yourselves, for if I were to explain it fully here we will go slightly off-topic and you probably won't believe what you are reading. Search for yourself what fractional reserve banking is, along with how fiat currency is created in the first place by your government and central bank, and you will be sorely disappointed.

Half a century later, this mentality of printing free currency (like it's going out of fashion) has escalated to a point where most countries are now massively in debt. So much so that the debt can never be repaid! But why is there a debt in the first place? Who does the government, meaning you and I, owe this debt to?[4] More uncertainty I'm afraid and to delve into this conspiracy is beyond the scope of this book and regardless of the truth and who benefits, one thing is for sure, the citizens suffer.

---

[4] Some people believe that the central banks are privately owned (or at least controlled by privately owned banks) and not in any way shape or form an official part of their respective governments, and that shareholders of the central banks are the only true beneficiaries of this system. As we the citizens pay the debt to the central banks via the governments.

Not only do our savings and pensions lose their worth through constant inflation (printing new currency), but our taxes increase to pay off the national debt and if required, our public services are cut. All this uncontrolled printing has meant that the once financially strong America is now in debt to the tune of an unbelievable 25 trillion dollars,[5] while the UK is ranked 5th in the global debt chart, with 2.8 trillion pounds of debt owed! These days we hear the words billions and trillions thrown around regularly and even flippantly. For those who are unsure how large a billion dollars or pounds is, it is a thousand, millions. While a trillion is a million, millions! Regardless of the currency and denomination of note or bill, all the debt created by the world's governments fiat currency printing would wrap itself around the earth multiple times. To be clear, I'm stating that our world debt, would create a wad of notes so large it would circumnavigate the world many times over. Quite literally choking us in debt!

A useful website to help visualise this debt is www.demonocracy.info where you can see a video and brilliant graphics showing what America's debt looks like laid out on football fields, and alongside the statue of liberty. You will be shocked when you see how vast 20 trillion dollars looks when laid out in million-dollar, metre squared cubes. Especially when you consider that the US dollar is still hanging by a thread as the global reserve currency and should it or any of its top banks or companies fail, the knock-on effect for the rest of the world could be catastrophic. Many analysts and independent commentators believe we are long overdue another correction in the financial markets. Similar to 2008 but now made a lot worse, predominately due to the world's governments overprinting of currency since then. According to *CNN Money London*, a whopping $9,000,000,000,000 (trillion)

---

[5] www.usdebtclock.org/world-debt-clock.html here you will see the 'debt clocks' of many countries rising in real-time!

has been printed by America, England, Japan, and the European central bank since the Great Recession of 2008. (That figure does not include the additional 'stimulus' we have seen since the coronavirus pandemic started). Also, you should note that the quantitative easing that started in 2008 continues to this very day, as only in late 2019 $500 billion was added to the US economy to stop the American Repo market from failing, which could have easily started a chain reaction of defaults and possible crashes across the country and even the planet.

As we can see, this was *before* the worldwide shutdown from the pandemic. Please remember that fact and know that the global economy had *not* recovered from the Great Recession.

Note that this printing of this additional currency has been rampant, continuous, and most worryingly has not improved the situation at all. In 2020 we have now seen many more trillions pumped into the global economy in response to the pandemic. Remember all this additional printing creates debt, debt that incurs interest and a debt that someone must pay back! Independent pundits believe all this extra printing of fiat currency since 2008 has only kicked the can down the road and will only make matters worse when the next crash comes.

The term that you may wish to search for regarding this subject would be *The Everything Bubble*. In 2008, it was an American real estate bubble bursting, which started the global financial crisis. Whereas this time there is believed to be a global real estate, stock market, bond market and currency bubble, all at the same time. This extra printing of worthless fiat has extended the dollar, euro, and pounds lifespan by an extra generation, but unfortunately many believe the end is in sight. Are the Chinese looking to capitalise on this situation? They have exceptionally large stockpiles of gold and silver which they are continually growing! It is plausible that over the coming years or decades they offer themselves to the world as a suitable candidate to provide a new reserve currency for us all. This will not happen overnight and would only happen once the US dollar steps (or falls) down. Like many things in recent history, this switch in dominance will be interesting to live through. Although the dollar has been the reserve currency for the world since the signing of the Bretton Woods agreement in 1944, we should not believe that this will always be the case. Before America held the torch, England had the global reserve currency. Before England, it was France, the Netherlands, Spain and then Portugal back in the mid-1400s. As you can see, this reserve currency status has been fluid for many centuries, and with America's debt in such a sorry state we should expect a new torchbearer to arise in the next few decades.

As this book is being finalised before going to print, we now see the world caught in the coronavirus pandemic.

Global economies ground to a halt and a worldwide depression looks inevitable. It now looks as if, courtesy of the virus, that *The Everything Bubble* will now burst. The word burst does not do the situation justice. Catastrophically explode like the Death Star is perhaps more fitting. Most of the people in this world will believe that the virus itself (or the associated shutdown) will have caused this. However, I believe that although the virus has not helped matters, the system was already failing. It was doomed to fail, arguably at the point of the US central bank's creation in 1913. Or after the two world wars, where more debt was written onto the balance sheets of all the world's citizens. If not then, it was certainly doomed when Nixon took the dollar completely off the Gold Standard, and if you don't think that is the case, then the final nail in the coffin has to be the additional QE of over $9 trillion since the Great Recession in 2008! The virus has not helped by a long shot, but the fiat currency system we find ourselves trapped in was never going to survive. Remember this additional $9 trillion has been trying to stop the global economy from imploding in on itself since 2008 with *no* positive effect! The global currency system, in my opinion, was only a few heartbeats away from flatlining.

This pandemic has sped up the final death rattle, and if nothing else will be used as a scapegoat as to why our beloved system has failed us. The virus will be the villain, and the true reason will never be spoken of. My only concern is how the world's governments and central banks will now react financially to this crisis. They have already stepped forward with 'extremely generous bailout and rescue packages'. All more debt, to add to the ever-growing pile of trillions and trillions that *we* must pay off, via increased taxes and reduced services. Again, many contrarian (alternative) thinkers, believe a sharp and brutal period of defaults would be preferable. Rescue the people, but maybe not the banks and large companies who were bailed out in 2008 and since then have carried on the exact same path they were on. No saving of capital to protect themselves, just more business as usual. Exorbitant bonuses for themselves and their shareholders, and using much of this newly created currency, to buy back their own stocks to become even wealthier.

As citizens, we are encouraged to have a 3-6 month emergency fund, ready for periods of unemployment and other eventualities. Why have many of these large and supposedly financially responsible and astute organisations, not protected themselves in a similar manner? Yes, I know this pandemic is an extreme situation, even unprecedented, (if you can bear hearing that word again) but many contrarian thinkers believe that the only way forward is to let all the irresponsible organisations fail. They will be bought up by businesses and entrepreneurs who have available capital and will be recirculated and hopefully transformed into even better companies. Machinery, equipment, workers, and their knowledge will not be wasted. Financially responsible people will see their opportunity and buy these assets and put them to good use. We bailed out the banks in 2008, basically rewarding their bad behaviour of the previous decades and by all accounts it looks like we are going to do the same again, reward their continued bad behaviour by enslaving ourselves to them and the central banks even more so.

The ramifications of the pandemic, the likely depression and the continuation of the fiat system (or its collapse) will keep us all tuned to our televisions and radios for many months and years to come. Those of us not familiar with the century-long con game will cry out to our politicians to help us by printing more currency, unaware that we are allowing the system to control us even more.

I apologise for a rather gloomy chapter. Can you see what fiat currency has done to us all? Yes, it paid for all the rebuilding after the Second World War, space exploration and some pretty cool decades from the counterculture of the 60s hippy era, through to the 80s and up to today. But deep down (and possibly without most people's realisation) it has mainly brought the world pain and suffering, through command and conquer. Let us now refocus our aim onto the purpose of this book, to learn about a radical new system that is separate from this ageing and crumbling legacy system. A system that is new and fresh and hopes to return humanity to a prosperous time. One that is fairer and gives power back to the people using it and has no shareholders and knows not of multimillion-dollar bonuses. A system that is strong and robust and will *never* need a bailout like fiat currency repeatedly looks for. Before we end this chapter and look forward to the future of finance, here are some wise quotes that may help to highlight what a sorry state our current financial system is in.

"It is well enough that people of the nation do not understand our banking and monetary system, for if they did, I believe there would be a revolution before tomorrow morning".
-Henry Ford (Founder of the Ford Motor Company).

"Who controls the issuance of money controls the government".
-Nathan Meyer Rothschild (Famous banking dynasty).

"Gold is money, everything else is credit".

-J.P. Morgan (Wealthy banker from the early 1900s).

"It is no coincidence that the century of total war coincided with the century of central banking".

-Ron Paul (Former American Congressman and presidential candidate).

"In the absence of the Gold Standard, there is no way to protect your savings from confiscation through inflation. There is no safe store of value. If there were, the government would have to make its holding illegal, as was done in the case of gold".

-Alan Greenspan. (Economist & Chairman of the Federal Reserve 1987-2006).

WE ARE ALL SATOSHI

B efore we dive headfirst into the subject of Bitcoin, let's learn a bit of the history and set a small but solid foundation so we can build a good understanding of what Bitcoin is and what it can offer.

But just before we do, there is a slightly confusing issue that we should quickly address. The Bitcoin network (the technology) *and* the currency used within the network, are both called Bitcoin. To try to make the distinction between the network and the currency, the community have tried to adopt a capitalisation technique. If we are talking about the network itself, the actual technology, then we capitalise the word Bitcoin. However, if we are referring to the currency, the actual units (the units of account/money) that are stored and spent on the Bitcoin network, then we drop the capital B and call them bitcoin with a lowercase b. Not terribly confusing, but I thought it was best that we clear that issue up as soon as possible and before we get too far into this book, and you wonder why I drop the capital B from time to time. To clarify one last time, big B equals the technology/network, little b the actual money.

Also, there is no plural of a bitcoin. You can own a fraction of a bitcoin, one or two bitcoin, or if you're very lucky twenty bitcoin. Notice how an 's' at the end of the word is not needed or required. There are no bitcoins, only bitcoin.

Bitcoin was announced to the world on Halloween 2008 and in early January 2009, the first-ever bitcoin transaction took place. Since then there have been hundreds of millions of transactions, ranging from a few pennies worth at a time to the largest of all transactions, that weighed in at 500,000 bitcoin (which at the time translated to nearly £80 million).[6]

Attached to the first-ever bitcoin transaction was a few words. These words were taken from the front cover of *The Times* newspaper on the 3rd January 2009. It serves as a timestamp to show when Bitcoin went live, but also appears to have had a secondary purpose. The words read 'Chancellor on brink of second bailout for banks'. This is in reference to the UK Chancellor of the Exchequer preparing to protect the British banks from failing on their debts. It is believed by many to show how the inventor of Bitcoin was unhappy with the banker bailouts and how in part, Bitcoin had been developed to offer the world a more stable, fairer alternative to the existing monetary system. One that could not be abused by anyone or any government.

Bitcoin was invented by a person (or persons) known as Satoshi Nakamoto. He, she, or they, developed Bitcoin after their dismay with how our modern banking system had been hijacked. They believed that government currency was not working in the people's favour and was being abused by the central banks that control the supply and interest rate. Satoshi worked in secret, most likely because he did not want to be arrested for creating a system that challenged the generations-old, financial behemoth. In April 2011 Satoshi sent a message stating he was "moving on to other things" and that "it's in good hands with Gavin and everyone". Gavin Andresen became the lead developer from that point and worked on Bitcoin until 2016. Since then, many other individuals have continued to help develop Bitcoin, but Satoshi has not been heard of since. Many people believe that Satoshi had to disappear, as eventually the authorities would have caught up with him and would have either co-opted him or forced him to

---

[6] In 2019 we had a transaction that was valued at £770 million ($1 billion), with 94,504 bitcoin being moved in a single transaction (when the price of a single coin was £7,700).

stop the project. Others believe that it would have strongly damaged Bitcoin if there was one person at the top who could have steered the technology like a dictator. This may sound very mysterious and the conspiracy theories are long regarding the creator of Bitcoin.

Some people believe he is a British individual, because of the language, phrases, and spelling of certain words he used, along with the times of the day he was active online. Other people believe Satoshi is now dead and one big piece of information to support this point is, that all of Satoshi's coins that she acquired in those early years have never moved. Numbers vary; however, many believe Satoshi has between 600,000 and 1,000,000 bitcoin. Once he, she or they walked away from the project, these coins have not moved and to this very day have been untouched. Every few months, a news article breaks claiming that the identity of Satoshi has been uncovered, but so far, all the stories have led to nothing. Some people believe that the NSA (National Security Agency) created Bitcoin.[7]

However, most people believe Bitcoin was not a secret government project and was created by citizens wishing to change the future for the better. Over the years many names have been put forward for being Satoshi. Two credible names often cited are Nick Szabo and Hal Finney. Szabo is a computer scientist and cryptographer who has given much to the community. He was also the developer of BitGold, a decentralised internet money that became the precursor to the Bitcoin architecture. Hal Finney was also a computer scientist who happened to be the first person to ever connect to the Bitcoin network after Satoshi. He also received the first-ever transaction when Satoshi sent him 10 bitcoin in a test

---

[7] In the early 1990s, they released a scientific paper on how the feat of creating a new type of digital currency could be achieved. Also, an integral part of Bitcoin, a computer function known as SHA-256, (Secure Hash Algorithm) is an NSA creation.

transaction. Unfortunately, the mystery of whether Hal Finney was Satoshi may never be solved as Hal sadly died of the disease ALS, more commonly known as motor neurone disease in 2014.

We may never know the identity of Satoshi or her motives or political beliefs. However, we do know the history of how Bitcoin adoption has evolved over these early years including the political persuasions of some of the first people to use this new money.

- The first people to use the technology were the cypherpunks. This was the self-given name for the group of cryptography experts, whose beliefs on security and privacy first spawned the search for a better monetary system. Szabo, Finney, and Satoshi were cypherpunks and members of the now-famous cypherpunk mailing list that many people refer to, where individuals discussed and theorised ways of designing a system like Bitcoin. Other cypherpunks that should be cited in this paragraph are David Chaum, Adam Back and Wei Dai. David Chaum was the first trailblazer and invented Ecash in 1983. Adam Back created Hashcash in 1997. Wei Dai developed B-money the following year. In 2004 Hal Finney made RPOW and Nick Szabo gave us BitGold in 2005. All these designs (for various reasons) either never left the drawing board, gained true traction, or were stopped before they could become adopted. These people are ultimately who we should thank for Bitcoin as they pushed the science and research, which allowed Satoshi to create it. Without detailing the history extensively, Satoshi took these earlier attempts to make an open and privacy-focused internet money and incorporated many of the technologies they had all used and built on top of them, added her own settings, functions, parameters, code and created Bitcoin.

- Hot on the heels of the cypherpunks were the anarchists and crypto-anarchists. Unfortunately, the meaning of the word anarchism has been skewed somewhat over the years. I have heard many anarchists speaking their opinions and theories and frankly, most of these individuals sound quite nice, grounded, and sensible. Yes, there may be some diehard anarchists out there, however, the majority have morals and beliefs that most people would happily agree with. Anarchy means the absence of government (the fire and chaos parts are optional and quite rare).

- Anarcho-capitalists were also quick to join the party. People who believe with many anarchist views but with a sprinkle of free-market philosophy thrown in for good measure. Along with the elimination of centralised state domination, in favour of self-ownership, private property and among many other things, natural law.

- When Bitcoin was still young, the next people to enter the community were the Libertarians (from the political philosophy Libertarianism). Their beliefs on autonomy (self-government) freedom of choice, voluntary association and individual judgment were well aligned with a decentralised and fair money.

- Around this time the customers of the infamous website *Silk Road* joined the new economy. Not everyone who uses any new technology is a saint and the media loved this negative angle in those early years. Silk Road was a marketplace where nearly anything could be purchased, a bit like an unregulated eBay with the only currency used on the site being bitcoin. Due to its decentralised model and libertarian swinging ethics, drugs could be purchased on the site. Contrary to reports at the time, many items were banned on the site. Items that could be used to hurt people such as weapons and items that included a victim, such as stolen data and IDs were not allowed to be sold.

Back in 2011, many people thought bitcoin transactions were completely private, so they were more than happy to use the new currency on this website believing their tracks would be concealed. (However, this is not the case, Bitcoin is *not* private). The full story is a fascinating one that cannot be covered fully here. Suffice to say the FBI finally tracked down the person running the site and he was arrested in a coordinated sting operation at a library. He turned out to be a peaceful and placid young man named Ross Ulbricht, who believed (as many others did) that he was making the streets safer for people. The judge thought the opposite and in what can only be described as a warning to others, sentenced the young, non-violent, first time offender to a double life sentence plus forty years with no chance for parole. Many Bitcoiners have since donated their currency of choice to the FreeRoss movement that his mother tirelessly operates. Over 160 prominent individuals and organisations have joined the hundreds of thousands of people that have signed a petition to get Ross released.[8]

- At each point in these early stages, many tech-focused individuals would have been hearing of this strange new digital version of gold and undoubtedly started to test, experiment, speculate and adopt the new technology. Poker players were also early users as they were forced to look for alternatives when their fiat deposits to their favourite gambling sites started to be hindered or even restricted.

- Many economists from the Austrian side of the economic divide started to join the community. These people (who are

---

[8] This includes Noam Chomsky (the American linguist and philosopher), Tom E. Woods (a libertarian historian, author and senior fellow from the Mises Institute), Jesse Ventura (former Navy frogman, US Governor and actor best known for playing Blain in the 1987 hit *Predator*) and among many others the actor Keanu Reeves (*The Matrix*).

opposed to the more establishment swinging, Keynesian economic theories), undoubtedly liked the fundamentals that Bitcoin brought to the table. Chiefly, a money that is backed by solid fundamentals, that being cryptography and maths, as opposed to flimsy government policies. Austrian economists are not people from Austria, the country. They are proponents of the Austrian school of economics that originated in *that* country from the economist Carl Menger and his 1871 book *Principles of Economics*. Other great minds joined the 'Austrians' such as Ludwig Von Mises, Friedrich Hayek and in more recent history, 1976 Nobel Prize winner Dr Milton Friedman and Murray Rothbard the prolific author, anarchist and Co-founder of the Mises Institute. Today the 'Austrian torch' is held globally by thousands of academics across the world. This includes fellows and members of the Mises Institute and includes such names as Lew Rockwell (another Co-founder of the Mises Institute), Tom E. Woods and former US Congressman Ron Paul. As a side note, you may be interested to learn that many 'Austrian thinkers' the world over, are also libertarians or anarchists. This might help to highlight that being an anarchist does not mean you are mentally unbalanced, as when you hear the reasoning and logic behind many of their theories, you may realise that thinking in such a way is quite rational (especially when you discover how inefficient and even dangerous governments can be).

- Then the early entrepreneurs and speculators joined the party. People who were interested in the financial possibilities of what Bitcoin could offer. These people had already seen or heard the stories of how a bitcoin was once worth fractions of a penny and had now rocketed past parity with the US dollar. As the community grew and people started to understand its design, it became plausible that its future price could easily climb to three, four or even five digits and more.

- Then the first big wave came, the first round of retail investors. People not too dissimilar from you and me. These people fuelled the price rise of 2013 where it peaked at nearly £1,000 per coin, bringing Bitcoin's name into pop culture forever. Banks, governments, and the media could no longer ignore it and there was no turning back.
  The media started a full-scale assault on Bitcoin with as much negative press as possible. Bitcoin was steadfast though. It knows nothing about good versus evil, or right and wrong. The coordinated onslaught lasted a good two to three years before its ferocity started to decline.
  Bitcoin's armour was thick, and it withstood the barrage of lies and misinformation. Now there is more of a news blackout than an orchestrated attack. These days, in the UK at least, it is exceedingly rare to see a television report on the subject. (I imagine they will return once the price rises above the previous all-time high). There are written articles from time to time and these are often negative.
  Still dredging up old and negative stories of exchanges being hacked, or people losing coins and scams.
  However, for those of us who keep our ears close to the ground, there is a constant stream of mainly positive news in the space. Unbelievable development and progress in this new industry that is taking place weekly, but the media by and large simply do not report it.

- The 2013 price fever bounced hard off the radar screens of the big boys, the institutional investors. Some of the smaller and more independent players and family offices started to enter the space shortly afterwards. While many of the bigger names held back, waiting to see how the story would develop. Would the world's governments quickly outlaw the technology? Many believe governments were too slow in learning what Bitcoin is and by not reacting quickly enough, they lost all chance of stopping it. So now, for the last year or so and building with every passing quarter, the big private investors, the hedge funds, asset management companies, exchanges, all the retail, commercial and investment banks, loan associations, sovereign wealth funds, governments and central banks are all either starting to buy or seriously asking the question, "when should we buy our first bitcoin"? Soon in the near future, it is plausible that these big players might legitimately see it as being very silly or even risky, not to have at least 1% exposure to this new digital commodity.

- Most of the public are still unsure what the crack is with Bitcoin, yourself included. That is why you purchased (or borrowed) this book, because you had a desire to learn more. The public by and large are still a few steps behind you and ignoring the elephant in the room. Soon the next big rush of Joe public is going to want to buy some bitcoin and then we could see adoption start to rise like never before.

"I see Bitcoin as ultimately becoming a reserve currency for banks, playing much the same role as gold did in the early days of banking. Banks could issue digital cash with greater anonymity and lighter weight, more efficient transactions".

- Hal Finney

BITCOIN IS OPEN SOURCE

Thank you for your patience. I am aware that I haven't started detailing what Bitcoin actually is just yet, but rest assured we will jump into that topic very soon. Now that you have learnt that Bitcoin was created in secret and that there are up to a million bitcoin still held by Satoshi, this may be concerning for some people. So, I thought now would be a good time to dispel some of those fears slightly, by talking about Bitcoin's open-source nature.

Open source means that the computer code within a program is public and viewable. Microsoft and Apple, for example, make operating systems that are used by millions of us, however, their software is not open source, it is closed. They do not want us and their competition seeing how they have designed their software. Most large companies will operate in the same fashion as they wish to keep the inner workings of their system secret. The inner workings, which they believe makes their product unique, special, secure or whatever the case may be. It is also believed by some people, that governments require companies to place 'back doors' into their software, (especially phone software) so that the governments themselves can easily pull data from our devices. This could be done for several reasons and if this is happening, we would like to think that it is not abused and is only used for serious reasons such as fighting terrorism. But if this is happening it could be leaving our devices open to prying eyes from other individuals, companies, and hackers. This highlights the need for extra care and security considerations when dealing with cryptocurrencies.

This is one of the main reasons why open source software has gained lots of traction over recent years. As it allows people to view the computer code and determine whether it is safe, with no back doors or malicious code running in the background. Bitcoin and its code have been reviewed by multiple experts the world over, in all the various disciplines that it employs and has been deemed safe. To date, there have only been a few bugs uncovered and when they were, the community of users and developers quickly rallied together and promptly fixed the issues. It is Bitcoin's open-source nature and the fact that no known vulnerability is present, which makes it trusted by so many people worldwide. Because there is no *one* person or company running Bitcoin, it is the responsibility of the developers, businesses and experienced users to aid the growth and development of the network. Individuals can submit a Bitcoin Improvement Proposal, known as a BIP. These get reviewed for their usefulness and if deemed necessary and safe, they are developed and implemented into the Bitcoin code. Many other cryptocurrencies operate in the same fashion, where community members can make suggestions or even submit their own computer code for review and implementation.

DISPELLING A FEW MYTHS

Before we get too deep into this book let's quash a few old myths. Bitcoin is a disruptive technology. Just as the motor vehicle was a disruptive technology if your livelihood revolved around the horse and cart. For this reason, it was feared and even hated by many people on their first encounter with it. These emotions have stayed for the people who feel it will destroy the equilibrium that they are accustomed to in their personal life or employment sector. Bitcoin was indeed developed to challenge the traditional financial system, but it would not be fair to say it was designed to destroy it. Myths and lies quickly spread when Bitcoin presented itself to the world. The first news reports that aired were almost comical. The media have done a fair job of trying to discredit and quash Bitcoin and to this very day still try their best to spin the news in the establishments' favour. Below are just a few long-since busted myths, so that you can hopefully sit back and absorb the rest of the information in this book more openly.

The Bitcoin CEO is dead. Bitcoin is not a company, there is no Managing Director or CEO! There is no leader or single person in charge of the project. Which in part, helps to make it decentralised, with no authority or single entity calling the shots. Being decentralised also means there is no single point of failure.

Bitcoin has no legitimate users. This is just not the case. There are millions and millions of legitimate users ranging from individuals to some rather large companies! It is *not* solely used for money laundering and other illegal activity, as the media might have led you to believe. There are undoubtedly many criminals using Bitcoin, however, I am convinced that the US dollar still holds that record and will do so for some time.

Surely we can't ban a technology because criminals use it. Unsavoury types use pounds and dollars, mobile phones, cars, shoes and even pencils. I don't hear politicians proposing that these items are banned.

Bitcoin is completely private. Untrue. Some identifiable information *is* recorded. Many newcomers believe Bitcoin is totally anonymous, but this is just not the case. Bitcoin is pseudonymous, meaning to some degree your identity is unknown, but do not think you are completely shielded or hidden. Transactions are publicly viewable, and governments and taxation agencies will for evermore be monitoring and analysing them. Many new companies specialise in what is called *blockchain analysis.* Through monitoring bitcoin transactions a picture, or a web of users and usage can be mapped out. The customers of these blockchain analysis firms will include governments and various three-lettered agencies such as the NCA, MI5, MI6, FBI, CIA, NSA, IRS and HMRC (oh hang on that's a four-lettered agency, well anyway you get the point).

Bitcoin is not safe and can be hacked! Many third-party companies, exchanges and individual users in the space have been hacked, but not Bitcoin itself. It is extremely secure. The 'bug bounty' for anyone who can find a weakness and hack Bitcoin is extremely high. This bounty is the total worth of all the bitcoin combined. This figure fluctuates but it is now over one hundred billion pounds. Quite an incentive you will agree! Many have tried to attack the network, some for the money and some to merely discredit Bitcoin. Either way, Bitcoin has stood the test of time and to date, nobody has cracked the science and maths that secures Bitcoin.

ENTER BITCOIN: A NEW MONEY FOR THE PEOPLE

Let's get this party started. So, what is Bitcoin? Depending on how deep or thorough an answer is expected, this is possibly one of the hardest questions to answer. As at every point in the answer, you may have to explain what is meant by a particular word or phrase. Bitcoin is a technology. In some respects, it is like the internet or even the file-sharing website BitTorrent (which allows people to share films and music files). However, instead of sharing data, as in the case of the internet, or film and music files in the case of BitTorrent, on the Bitcoin network people can share bitcoin. Special pieces of data that have been specially designed to behave and act like real money. At its most basic layer, Bitcoin is just another protocol (system of rules) that sits on top of the internet, just like email. One entrepreneur in the space, Erik Voorhees, sums up Bitcoin in a few worthy lines. "I think Bitcoin is a prism through which people see the world in different ways. It's really a hydra, people see different things in it. Just like the internet. What is the internet? Well, it's different things to different people. That's the sign of a truly transformative technology". Satoshi also had an interesting way of explaining Bitcoin to new people, he said "Imagine finding a new element on the periodic table. A new element that has all the same qualities as gold, however, this new element has one property that gold doesn't have, that it can be transmitted over the internet. That's what Bitcoin is, a modern version of gold that can be transported electronically".

For many years people have attempted to make digital money that could be sent over the internet, independently and directly between two people. A type of money that was decentralised, meaning it is not controlled by any one person, country, government or central bank. A type of money that is designed fairly and was not going to be overproduced or inflated. Simply put, bitcoin is that new money! It is stored on our computers and phones and is sent over the internet, a bit like an email. Just because it lives on computers and phones and moves over the internet, do not be confused and think it is no different to our current 'digital' government currency and the multitude of different banking apps and payment services such as Apple/Samsung Pay and PayPal, as it is worlds apart from our traditional currency and these services. If I were to try to make an analogy with aeroplanes, then fiat currency and these services are a wooden framed plane, powered by a gentleman with a rather bushy moustache sat on what looks like a bicycle. While Bitcoin is quickly evolving into a modern jet, capable of breaking the speed of sound, skimming the edge of space and performing loop the loops! One big selling point or feature of Bitcoin is that a transfer is possible without the need of a trusted third party such as Visa, Mastercard, HSBC, Barclays, Western Union and PayPal. All the institutions just mentioned use the global payment network, *The Society for Interbank Financial Telecommunications* known as SWIFT. It handles most of the world's financial messaging, weighing in at around $5 trillion per day. Bitcoin does not need any centralised organisation to operate. This concept of no trusted third party being required is quite important, so I shall repeat it: Bitcoin allows users to send digital money, or value over the internet to one another, without the need for a middleman, no bank or institution is needed. That last sentence is one of the primary reasons why Bitcoin is seen by so many people as revolutionary! If we think about it, it is in some ways similar to how email removed the middleman from us communicating with one another. Originally we needed stagecoaches, trains, and aeroplanes to transport our physical letters to one another which birthed the Royal Mail as we know it today. Email allowed for faster correspondence to take place and for it to be done directly between ourselves and at a fraction of the cost.

Bitcoin is 100% digital, with no physical coins or notes. Some people like to call it digital gold or gold 2.0, while others prefer the term digital asset. Because it is based around computer code, another term used is programmable money. Just focus on that thought for a moment. Money that can be designed and programmed with a computer to behave as you wish. Wow, just imagine what the future could entail if money were designed to behave fairly from the start. If it was not directly controlled by anyone, not a central bank or even a government (that may not have your best interest at heart). But that it was designed by citizens and was designed to behave in a set and predictable way, and should you agree with these set principles, then you would be free to enter and leave this new economy at will. Well, that future is here, and it is developing at a lightning pace.

Bitcoin is the world's first cryptocurrency, aka crypto for short. It is called a cryptocurrency because it uses the science of cryptography to secure the payments along with people's wallets, which is the new term for an account (see Appendix A). We will learn more about cryptography in the next part of this book. For now, all we need to know is that cryptography is a very secure way of transmitting electronic data. All the data that relates to Bitcoin is stored within a new type of technology called a blockchain. For the moment we can visualise a blockchain as being a very large and extremely secure, tamper-proof and publicly viewable digital spreadsheet. As you may already see, Bitcoin is vastly different from the digital banking system we are accustomed to. We will look at both cryptography and blockchains in the next part of this book so let's not get too hung up on these terms just yet.

Bitcoin is also distributed, as there are thousands of computers, called nodes (see Appendix A) spread around the world running the Bitcoin software. These nodes store the Bitcoin blockchain (data) and propagate the transactions across the network. Because there are many of these nodes, there is strength in numbers, as if one were to fail or leave the network there is no disruption to any security or level of service. Many of these nodes are owned by regular individuals, who wish to help Bitcoin flourish. Other node operators will include businesses and exchanges within this new industry. This distributed network of computers helps to secure and manage Bitcoin. So, if no company or individual is in charge, who runs Bitcoin? The Bitcoin software itself is what controls and manages Bitcoin, while maintaining the software and the network is left to an unpaid army of cryptography experts, computer scientists, software developers and individuals that work on behalf of the people that use Bitcoin.

Another reason Bitcoin is seen as such a groundbreaking invention is because of its censorship-resistance. This can be described in two different ways:

- Once a transaction has been processed and is included in the blockchain (spreadsheet/database) it cannot be removed or altered. Nobody can censor that transaction or alter the history of it. This is quite a big deal, as it allows for a totally honest and transparent payment system to exist for the first time in history. No third party is needed to verify transactions, the transactions are permanently recorded and undeletable, meaning users can authenticate transactions themselves. No bank or authority is needed.

- It is also censorship-resistant in that anybody can join and use the Bitcoin network. There is no government, bank or third party that censors or controls who can or cannot open a wallet (account) and operate within the network. People are free to use Bitcoin at their own will. Young children can open a wallet just as easily as the hundreds of millions of people who are denied bank accounts around the world. Whether that is the homeless or certain people from certain persuasions, demographics, religions, professions or any other group or sub-group that can be censored or downtrodden. Bitcoin is computer code and does not care who you are or who you are associated with. If you have a phone or PC and the relevant software you are welcome. In this sense, Bitcoin can also be described as being permissionless.

It has been the aim of many people over the last forty years to develop a monetary system that enabled individuals to send money (or digital value) over the internet to each other independently. There have been many attempts, but they all failed for various reasons. This has been partly due to there always being a company or individual at the top, which the governments or financial regulators could stop or arrest. Experts in the field of cryptography believed that their discipline would be the way that the goal would be achieved. However, much work was needed as the barriers to overcome were still very high. A small subset of cryptography experts, the aforementioned cypherpunks, were the group most focused on this mind-boggling task. They worked for years, trying to crack the science required to enable the creation of a frictionless, permissionless, payment network for the people. One that could bypass the traditional systems and allow for the first time in history, the ability for the public to send digital money to each other over the internet without the need for a trusted third party.

One problem with digital information is that it can be easily copied. If I were to send you a digital photo or mp3 music file via the internet, two copies now exist. There is nothing to stop you copying it again and again, sending multiple copies to other people. One breakthrough with Bitcoin is the ability to know that these digital assets cannot be copied, they have digital uniqueness! This may be a little hard to appreciate as we are now in a digital age, where everything is copiable but trust me, 'bitcoins' *cannot* be copied. The holder of the asset is the owner, and once sent to another individual, the sender no longer retains a copy or any claim/ownership. Once you receive bitcoin you can rest assured that you are now the owner and the sender cannot get it back, unless you choose to send it back to them.

Our regular banking system can be described as a 'pull network'. Where banks and companies can pull funds (normally with our consent) from our current accounts which are known as standing orders and direct debits. Cryptocurrency works oppositely and is known as a 'push network'. You are your own bank and in complete control. You decide when to push your cryptocurrency from your wallet.

As with lots of new technology, there are terms that many users may wish to learn, cryptocurrency is no different. One task for any new user will be to further their knowledge. This will most likely be done by visiting forums or watching videos on the internet, reading more material or listening to podcasts on the subject. Either way, you will quickly start to uncover terminology that is new to you. As cryptocurrency is still very new, with most users being computer geeks, teenagers and younger adults, some of the terms are a little stranger than one might expect. Either way, these still describe important facets of cryptocurrency that should be understood. At the back of this book, Appendix A has a list of many words that a beginner may wish to learn.

WHAT DOES A BITCOIN LOOK LIKE?

Satoshi Nakamoto designed bitcoin to have similar qualities to gold. There will be a finite or limited number of bitcoin and this cap is set to 21 million coins. Currently, there are over 18 million already in circulation (over 85% of the total supply).[9]

A single bitcoin has eight decimal places, this means there are eight zeros after the decimal point. One bitcoin reads as follows: 1.00000000 and as we well know, pounds, dollars and euros have only two decimals, which makes them divisible by 100 pence or cents. With a bitcoin having a far greater number of decimal places, it makes them much more divisible than fiat currencies. There are 100 million units within a *single* bitcoin. The nickname given to the smallest unit within a bitcoin is a Satoshi, and it is abbreviated to sat or s (and it looks like this 0.00000001). Many people decide not to invest or buy any bitcoin because they believe they have missed out on the early opportunities as they are now too expensive and they cannot afford to buy a whole bitcoin, or that you can only purchase them in complete units. Remember though that this asset is highly divisible so you *can* buy small amounts or fractions at a time. Depending on the fees associated with the exchange you use, buying small amounts of £30 or even less is common.

Within the community, there have been a couple of pushes over the years to change the mindset and terminology of how people denominate bitcoin. In essence, to abandon talking of bitcoin in their large, singular units and instead to 'count' in milli-bits (0.001), or in bits (0.000001) or even in Satoshi's (0.00000001).

---

[9] New coins are currently released to the network at the rate of 6.25 bitcoin every ten minutes. However, as we shall later learn, this figure will keep on reducing for many years to come, meaning it will take a long time for the remaining coins to be produced.

This would help to show members of the public that these coins are highly divisible and that they are not priced out of the average person's reach. For example, if one bitcoin was £10,000 many of us feel instantly priced out of this new technology, whereas if we were to refer to bitcoin (and its price) in milli-bits (a thousandth of a bitcoin), then one milli-bit (0.00100000) is only £10. Referred to in this denomination, people may feel more comfortable in buying/investing, as they no longer seem so expensive. To highlight how as humans, we do not like to price high-cost items in large denominations, we can think of how very few jewellers and investors price gold by the metric ton. If they did, everyone (who did not understand the maths at least) could be scared off by its price, as a ton of gold currently costs around £50 million. When the jeweller buys a small amount of gold to make a client's wedding ring they don't buy 0.000004 of a ton, they buy 4 grams worth. For this reason, gold is sold and priced in ounces and even grams. A much more suitable denomination you would agree, especially for a commodity that is so highly-priced. As Bitcoin's worth increases we may well see the same move, to talk and price this new digital commodity in smaller units. Be that milli-bits, bits or one day even in single Satoshi's. Just make a mental note that they are highly divisible with 100 million Satoshi's in a single bitcoin and that even if the price of a single bitcoin rises to 50 grand or more, we can still purchase small, comfortable amounts.

WHERE CAN WE USE THEM?

The places where bitcoin is accepted is growing every month. Originally, however, they were just passed back and forth between people to test the Bitcoin network. They were slowly becoming recognised as being special, and their future value to humanity was starting to materialise, however, they arguably had not yet gained any real price. The first recorded, real-world use of bitcoin (the one that kicked the price discovery into gear) took place on May 22nd, 2010 when Laszlo Hanyecz paid for two large Papa John's pizzas with bitcoin. Spawning the Bitcoin holiday, celebrated on that date every year, Bitcoin Pizza Day! He posted his request to buy pizza on a Bitcoin forum. He stated he didn't want to do anything except receive delivery of the pizza. He did not mind if it was takeaway or home-cooked pizza but stipulated it needed to be delivered directly to his home, preferably with enough to last until the following day. How much did Laszlo pay for the two pizzas? Well remember that it was ten years ago, and a bitcoin was only worth a fraction of a penny at the time. These two pizzas were purchased for 10,000 bitcoin! Yes, that's right 10,000. I know we shouldn't do the maths but let's anyway. Bitcoin's price fluctuates as we know, and at the time would have only amounted to forty-odd pounds, but taken at the height of the 2017 market, 10,000 bitcoin cost around £140 million.

We should not make fun of his purchase, remember Bitcoin was very new at that time and nobody knew how it would be adopted. Somebody had to start using it, and nobody can say that Laszlo would or could have retained all those coins since he first acquired them. Everyone has a price they intend to sell at, and the thought that he could have held all 10,000 coins over the intervening years and then been able to sell at the highest price is extremely slim. I just hope the pizza was tasty and that there was some leftover for the next day. Laszlo is still in the space so one can only assume he has collected some more sats.

Nearly ten years later, bitcoin is becoming more accepted with over 15,000 small independent businesses and some rather large companies currently accepting it. A list of some of the big players includes Microsoft, Rakuten, PayPal, Shopify, Wikipedia, (some Starbucks and Subways), Virgin Galactic (for those pioneering space tourists), Bloomberg, KFC in Canada, Etsy, Fiverr and WordPress. In the UK there are over 150 online stores that accept bitcoin. This number is continually growing as more people discover the technology along with its benefits. Physical locations in the UK that accept bitcoin are still limited, but two chains that do are Your Sushi and some BMW dealerships. Other independent stores across the country range from a coffee shop in Exeter to a chippy in Manchester. For a more extensive list of places that accept bitcoin in the UK you can visit: www.wheretospendbitcoins.co.uk or www.coinmap.org which shows bitcoin-accepting places across the world on a nice visual map and also includes the locations of Bitcoin ATMs. That's right, for a few years now we have Bitcoin ATMs (automated teller machines) which allow people to insert government currency and out pops decentralised cryptocurrency).

One big point to consider is that Bitcoin is a *peer to peer* payment system and that its adoption cannot solely be graded by how many shopkeepers and online businesses accept it. It is a means for individuals to pay one another 'privately' and for this reason, we must consider that people can and are using it to pay one another for all manner of reasons, from settling personal debts, tipping, freelance work and for money remittance (where individuals working abroad send money home to family members). It is fair to say that Bitcoin is still not universally accepted online or on the high street and that adoption by the general public is far from being in full swing.

Many people believe taxation and regulatory uncertainty is one big factor in stifling business adoption, however, one of the big payment processors called BitPay, recently announced they processed $1 billion worth of bitcoin for their merchants in 2019. Remember the technology is still relatively new and that the adoption of the internet also took many years. However, all these years later we can't imagine living our lives without constant internet connections to all our devices. Having said all this, Bitcoin has evolved quite a bit since its invention.

Some people are starting to hold onto the asset more than they spend it, as slowly people are realising that its future price could be much greater than it currently is today. Because of this, bitcoin is seen by some people as an asset, one that can be held for the long term to store value, a little bit like how someone might want to buy shares or even gold, to be used later in life. Others are buying it to hedge against economic downturns.

Before we start talking about bitcoin's price maybe now would be an appropriate time to include a short sentence to remind the reader that I am not a financial advisor, and that nothing in this book should be taken as personal, financial or investment advice. The reader is expected to undertake additional learning and seek the advice of professionals before spending or investing their government-issued currency, and that if you didn't read the disclaimer at the start of the book, maybe now would be a good time to flick back to the beginning and read it.

WHY ARE THEY WORTH SO MUCH?

This is a very subjective question. For some people, bitcoin is nothing more than worthless 'funny money' with no intrinsic value whatsoever. Some people may argue that a particular abstract painting is worthless or certainly not worth the asking price, while others will happily pay large sums to own it. 'One man's junk is another man's treasure' as the saying goes. There is possibly only one correct statement that can be made about all transactions the world over, regardless of the goods, currencies or commodities involved. That is, that both parties involved value the other person's goods more highly. It is obvious that both parties feel that they are getting (on some level) a good deal, otherwise few of us would trade our currency for goods as we do. The painter, for example, views your currency more valuable than they do their art supplies and time, while the buyer values the piece of art more than they do their own currency.

It is my opinion that value is subjective. Because of this reason, it is very hard to convince someone that any particular item has value. Just like beauty, value is in the eye of the beholder. We all have our own opinions and beliefs that help us mentally construct what we believe value is, and from that starting point, we can then assign, in varying degrees, values to the various items around us. Another thought is that someone might class an item as valuable but know they are never going to be able to afford it, and for this reason, it is off their radar, and they are simply not interested. Just as many of us may want a five-bedroom house with a pool, but few of us will ever be able to afford one. While at the other end of the stick, there can even be psychological and even societal hang-ups that prevent some people from having an interest or desire to buy or invest in certain items. One example of this is that everyone knows that silver and gold have value, but just how much value?

In our Western societies, few people value these metals unless it is in the form of jewellery. It is not valued enough by the general public to buy bullion coins for example. While in many countries, especially India and China, gold is highly valued and is regularly given to family members as gifts in its many different forms, from jewellery and tableware to ingots and coins.

For millions of users, Bitcoin has value for lots of reasons. People may not agree with many or any of these reasons. In no particular order, some reasons why Bitcoin has value:

- Bitcoin is the largest, decentralised monetary system to ever exist. It is (as far as we know) immutable and censorship-resistant.

- The Bitcoin network's computational power is the largest of any network on the planet.

- Dozens of developers have worked tirelessly on improving both the functionality as well as the user experience.

- Currently holding bitcoin, you can send that digital asset to any corner of the world, almost in an instant. It allows for the first time, an open, borderless and global payment network to exist.

- There are already millions of people who use it and over 400 million transactions have been made in total. It recently overtook PayPal in daily transactional volume, is PayPal considered valuable to its shareholders?

- The Bitcoin blockchain has shown it can perform well at transferring and storing digital value for us and we also now know it could be used to hold other sensitive data for us if we wish (such as medical records or house deeds).

- Its current supply is precisely known and can be projected out for decades in advance. There is no ambiguity on how many there will be at any given point in the future.

For example, we know (almost) exactly how many there will be in circulation at any random point in the future, say in nine years and four months! A feat that nobody can perform for dollars or pounds.

- Its supply is not only regulated, but it is slowing down. We also know the total supply is fixed. Estimates are vague but at least four million bitcoin are believed to be forever lost, making them scarcer than ever and to buy a tiny fraction of this powerful and world-changing technology, all you need to do is buy some bitcoin. Whether that's £100 or £10,000 worth, in owning even a fraction of a bitcoin, you could argue that you own a share or a percentage of this new global financial network. There are probably many more, but these are some of the main reasons why I and others believe Bitcoin has value.

WHY IS THE PRICE OF BITCOIN
EXPECTED TO RISE?

Bitcoin is designed to behave differently to our current monetary system. One big difference is that bitcoin will not be overproduced like pounds or dollars are. Only 21 million bitcoin will ever be made. Once the cap of 21 million is reached, production will stop. One interesting fact to note about this relatively low number is, that all the world's millionaires will not be able to own a *whole* bitcoin, as there are an estimated 30 million, millionaires on the planet. Imagine that for just one moment. That even if they wished, all the world's millionaires and billionaires could not own one bitcoin. The inventor also designed Bitcoin so that these coins would be slowly released, a bit like how gold is slowly mined from the earth. New bitcoin are released to the network roughly every ten minutes.

The amount released every ten minutes also decreases over time and is currently set at 6.25 bitcoin. This means that the *last* fraction of the very *last* bitcoin, will not be mined until the year 2140. However, 99% of all 21 million bitcoin will be in circulation by 2032! That's right, it will take over 100 years for the last 1% of all the available bitcoin to be produced.

Bitcoin is a new technology that has only recently become a household name. There is lots of speculation in this new market, but people are realising that bitcoin is in short supply. This scarcity will play a big factor with regards to bitcoin's price over the coming years.

Why has the price gone up so much in the last few years? More adoption and lots of speculation. Simply put, more people are hearing about it and many are downloading a wallet and buying a few pounds worth. Your average Joe 'investor' is referred to as a retail investor while the big companies and specialist investment firms and hedge funds are referred to as institutional investors. Most people who bought bitcoin from

2012-2018 were retail investors. Now slowly the institutional money is entering the space. There are still lots of people in both camps sitting on the side-lines but slowly the tide is turning. Some people who can see the future benefits are now buying what they can afford every month. Some people are buying it to preserve their wealth before government over-printing erodes their savings. Some people in developing countries, with economies far worse than ours, are also starting to use Bitcoin and other cryptos to protect themselves, as their government currency is losing its value day by day. Millions of pounds, dollars, euros, yen, pesos, won and shekels (to name but a few currencies) have been flooding into Bitcoin every month, from teenagers and techies, through to investors, day traders and even some large companies who all want a piece of the crypto pie. Many wealthy individuals, celebrities and sportsmen and women are also jumping in. For one reason or another, more and more people are buying bitcoin. In the latter half of 2017 alone, during the height of the last bull market, over 50,000 new Bitcoin wallets were opened every month.

Most of the people on the planet are underbanked. This Means they do not have full access to either bank accounts or banking services (like credit or loans) that we take for granted in the Western world. They too are discovering what Bitcoin and other cryptocurrencies can do for them. Bitcoin is also showing us here in the developed world how our current monetary system is broken. If not broken, it is not behaving like a well-greased and finely tuned machine, nor is it working in the favour of the common man or woman. Ask yourself how much purchasing power the British pound (or your fiat currency of choice) has lost over the last 100 years? Or since you were born or became aware of prices rising? Remember increased prices is a by-product of inflation, the cost of your cheese and butter hasn't necessarily gone up. Our currency has been devalued through overprinting which makes it worth less than it was. The knock-on effect of this means it takes more pounds, dollars, or euros to buy the item in question. I'm sure that if you investigate, you will be shocked when you discover how much value your currency has lost in the last 100 years. We all collectively have trillions and trillions of non-payable debt pounds and dollars stacking up for our children's children to pay off. Is this why, courtesy of the media and our politicians, we are slowly being accustomed to the word austerity? All these reasons above may help Bitcoin's price to rise over the coming decades, as more and more people see the benefits of Bitcoin and the disadvantages to the traditional system.

Figure 1 below is a chart from www.coinmarketcap.com showing the price of bitcoin in pounds from 2013 to 2020. We can see the relatively small blip (very early in the chart) when the price sharply climbed to an unbelievable amount at the time and nearly hit £1,000! The price then corrected and settled at around £250, where it bounced sideways for nearly four years. Then we had the meteoric rise to £15,000, which quickly crashed once the 2017 crypto fever passed. It eventually retraced 80% from the high and for some time bounced around the £3,500 mark. Recently the bitcoin price has started to climb again with many analysts now believing we have entered a new bull market. Now it looks like £5,000 Bitcoin could become a distant memory with many people believing £20,000 + is inevitable. With global daily volume being counted in the billions of pounds, it's fair to say there's still lots of interest.

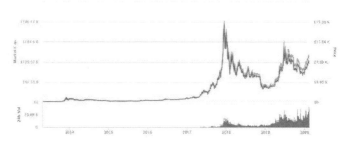

Figure 1. Bitcoin price chart

WHAT WILL A BITCOIN BE WORTH
IN THE FUTURE?

Please remember that nothing written in this book is financial or investment advice. Walk away from anyone who is sure what the price of a bitcoin will be next month. Chances are they don't know too much at all. Run away from anyone advising that you should invest your life savings into bitcoin, or to re-mortgage your home! Nobody knows what the price will do next week, let alone next year or the coming decades. Many people believe a single bitcoin will hit over £20,000 shortly. Predictions of £100,000 within a few years have been made by some, while others believe a single Bitcoin will eventually hit £1,000,000 with a few people believing they will be worth much more. It all comes down to how much fiat will be moved from the traditional financial markets into bitcoin, and that figure is anyone's guess. At the start of 2020, a report detailing the best and worst-performing assets of the last decade surfaced. (The bitcoin price at the start of 2010 is unclear, so the validity of the final figure quoted here is up for debate). Oil was the worst-performing commodity, dropping 26% over the ten years, with gold being the best commodity, rising 34%. (£1 invested in gold back then would now be worth £1.34). Bitcoin was in a league of its own, as £1 invested into bitcoin in 2010 would yield £90,000 in 2020. That is a 9,000,000% increase. (If nine million percent is not correct, its percentage gain would still likely be counted in multiple millions). Note that this type of return is *not* to be expected over the next decade and that readers should not look to invest in bitcoin until they are fully aware of the risks involved.

We have learnt that bitcoin is likened by many people as a new type of digital gold. So, let us look at gold, the money of kings and see how bitcoin's price could rise. The global gold market is currently worth around £5.6 trillion. If Bitcoin were to siphon off just 5% of that market, it could give each bitcoin a value of approximately £25,000. So, what if Bitcoin also took a 1% share away from the global stocks and shares industry, weighing in at around £53 trillion? Well, that could give bitcoin a price of around £60,000 per coin. Or how about including 1% of the global derivatives market (a whopping £400 trillion). That could equate to a price of roughly £250,000 per bitcoin! As you can see, it is quite plausible that if mass adoption starts and even a small percentage of traditional investment money is moved, the price of this digital asset could start to climb. The above figures only account for the gold, stocks and derivatives markets and do not include your average person or even institutions buying bitcoin with government currency. The link below will take you to a website which shows a brilliant visualisation of all the world's currency and how it is divided up between various sectors. We can only imagine what bitcoin's price will be if just a small percentage of the world's currency moves over to the new digital economy. Interestingly, it also shows Bitcoin in the chart and it is funny to see how small Bitcoin currently is compared to the other giants like gold, global real-estate and the derivatives market. https://money.visualcapitalist.com/worlds-money-markets-one-visualization-2017/

The primary reason any asset rises in value is because of the fine balance between supply and demand. Obviously, if nobody wants an item then its price will probably drop. In the same vein, if the item or commodity is overly abundant then likewise the value will likely go down. However, if there is demand and a low supply then prices can soar. Think of house prices in central London or any other metropolis for that matter. Space for new housing is not increasing, but the demand to buy a house and live there is steadily growing, therefore the house prices can climb. According to data from the building society Nationwide, 50 years ago the average house price in London was £12,800 whereas now it is nearly half a million. But, if everyone suddenly decided London was no longer the place to be, you could bet that house prices would fall and then rise in the next town or city that everyone wished to live. How does this balance of supply and demand relate to Bitcoin? We shall look further at the Bitcoin supply in the next part of this book, but to briefly show you how bitcoin's price may well rise substantially over the coming years and decades, we need to become aware of a function known as the Bitcoin halving (aka halvening). This simple but clever feature of how Bitcoin is managed means that every four years the supply of newly created bitcoin is reduced by 50%. This is governed by the Bitcoin code and happens automatically and will continue until all 21 million coins are released. In a nutshell, this function will drastically reduce the Bitcoin inflation rate until in the far future, Bitcoin's inflation rate hits 0%. While this steady decrease occurs, if the demand for bitcoin remains the same and especially if it increases, it can only do one thing, and that is to increase the price. This function is in some ways similar to how gold mining is becoming harder and harder to perform, as over the last couple of thousand years and especially the last century with our modern machinery, all the easy pickings have already been mined. Now the mining companies must dig deeper and deeper to tap into the gold veins.[10] Satoshi designed Bitcoin to mimic the rare and sort after qualities of commodities like gold and oil.

Another point to consider is that we are soon going to see a shift in which generation earns the highest wage. We are slowly transitioning from Gen Xs earning the most and starting to see the rise of the Millennials. Many of these Millennials along with the current generation, the Gen Zs, have become wary and even

---

[10] The World Gold Council believe that in a few short years more gold will be recycled than mined from the earth. The global oil supply is also believed to be reducing with fewer wells being found today. Wells that are found are generally much smaller and harder and more expensive to tap into.

disenfranchised by the big institutions of this world, be that banking and to some extent politics. They have also grown up in a solely digital era and are becoming quite aware of the importance of privacy through the constant barrage of data breaches and online security foul-ups. Some people believe that they may well park their surplus currency into a decentralised system like Bitcoin more readily than the generations before them. Also, we are seeing the Baby Boomer generation slowly retire and sadly die off. It is estimated that $59 trillion of fiat currency will filter down globally to Gen Xs and Millennials by 2060. This will be the largest transfer of wealth we have ever seen as the Baby Boomers are the wealthiest generation in human history. This may also have a big effect on the bitcoin price, as these younger generations try to protect their inheritance in this fairer and more decentralised way of storing wealth. Not only are people wanting to protect themselves from 'confiscation through inflation' as Alan Greenspan called it, but also to protect against a system that is almost designed/expected to fail every generation and also one that by law, can take currency directly from your accounts (if it can save a failing country) as we saw in the case of Cyprus only a few years ago. If you think that was a one-off random and freak occurrence and it wouldn't ever happen in *your* country, then please think again. In a disgusting show of disregard for the citizens of the world, this is often referred to as a *haircut*. We are told our current accounts here in the UK are protected up to £85,000 and in the US $250,000 but I believe these protection schemes or laws are probably not worth the paper they are written on. The terminology used to describe this blatant theft is very crafty, and people from generations before us would not have fallen for such a blatant con and infringement of our rights. It shows how politics and the media have done such a number on the people, as in years gone by, when someone stole or unfairly took money from someone it was called fleecing. Fleecing or a haircut, it's the same thing! We can now legally be stripped (or shaved like a sheep) of our savings! This is one of the many reasons Satoshi made Bitcoin and also time stamped a certain headline from *The Times* newspaper into the very start of the Bitcoin blockchain... 'Chancellor on brink of second bailout for banks'.

We will have a better understanding of bitcoin's future price as time goes on and as the cryptocurrency markets mature. I believe it will always be worth something and will never go to zero. As for a top-end figure, I cannot comment. I do think there is a lot more growth to come, but it would be unwise of me to fuel price speculation here. Governments can hinder crypto in many ways and whenever they choose. The UK government has not openly made its opinion known either way, although the US President recently voiced his dislike for the currency. A 2017 US senate hearing by the American financial regulators did go very well. My thoughts are that Bitcoin specifically is here to stay. Governments will for evermore be monitoring the Bitcoin blockchain and will be watching adoption closely. The UK and US governments will also want to collect capital gains and income taxes from crypto workers, investors, and traders and who knows, they may even soon start using the technology themselves. One plus that helps to cement the likelihood that Bitcoin is here to stay, is that many politicians and policy-makers are thought to now own bitcoin themselves, and as a result of this they would not want to hinder their own investments too much.

IT'S TOO LATE TO BUY ANY BITCOIN

This short chapter is not meant to frustrate the reader. Nobody, (myself included) likes to be told what to do with their money or how to spend it and this is not my intention. I only wish to make some of the readers of this book think a little about their spending and saving (or lack thereof). "It's too late to buy any bitcoin". This is probably the most common statement that I hear some friends and family proclaim. Many people spent the first few years bashing Bitcoin, but now that it has gained value and some respect, many of them feel it is too late to join the party. Almost as if showing an interest now, would be like admitting they were wrong to dismiss it all those years ago. As I mentioned earlier, some people see no value in Bitcoin. Others feel that they have missed the opportunity because they are now too expensive, and they cannot afford to buy a whole one. When you explain that a bitcoin is highly divisible (with 100 million units in each coin) and that they can buy small amounts and slowly over time, build up their position or portfolio, they might just shrug their shoulders and say something like, "well I would only want a whole one. There's no point in buying small amounts". Remember, all the world's millionaires will not be able to own a complete bitcoin. So obviously, the entire world's population is in the same boat. If global adoption does occur, everyone will only ever own fractions of a bitcoin. So, if you can appreciate this point, and you do see utility in this digital commodity, maybe now is the time to buy your fraction of bitcoin. The argument that a commodity that can be purchased in small quantities is somehow out of reach (for most people) is a weak one in my opinion. It is fair enough if they truly have no interest in the commodity, or no interest in saving for the future in any way, however, I believe most people *do* have the ability to save, even if it's just small amounts here and there.

Get a savings jar/piggy bank, either store-bought or just an old coffee jar, collect all your loose change or pound coins. Start a swear jar (if you dare) and see what kind of savings you can generate if only for a month or two. These days many apps can also help people save. One such app in the UK is called Chip. It will periodically save small amounts of fiat on your behalf. Another UK app that will round up your card purchases to the nearest pound and save the difference is called Moneybox. Chime and Qapital are two American savings apps. Then, once you have some savings, you can look at the ways of putting this fiat currency to a slightly better use, be that paying off debts or mortgages quicker, education, a pension, other investments or even bitcoin or gold. The list is large of the sensible things a percentage of our disposable income can be used for. Unfortunately, many of us just focus on the things that give us instant pleasure or gratification such as cinema tickets, video games, new clothes, beer or whatever your passions may be. As we shall see in the next chapter, the concept *time preference* plays a big part in how we view and use our currency and it also plays a big role in why many of us do not save or plan for the future, but just bumble along in the present, spending all of our fiat currency quickly before our new pay cheque arrives.

Yes, it is highly unlikely that anyone buying small amounts of bitcoin today is going to become a multi-millionaire or billionaire from their initial investment (unless you buy half a million or billion pounds worth today, with the belief that the price will double in the next few months or years), but that should not stop people learning about or even entering the new economy. This book is filled with positive reasons why people may want to join this future economy. Becoming rich may be one of those reasons but it isn't the be-all and end-all of the matter. Protecting your savings is one good reason, hedging your financial risk could be another. I personally do not see buying bitcoin…as buying. I see it as transferring currency from a devaluing pound and restoring it in a newer, fairer alternative.

One that all things willing, will appreciate over the years. It is never too late to start saving (or buying bitcoin), just as it is never too late to learn a new skill. If I could turn back time, I would take great advantage of my new understanding of how saving for the future would be a good idea. I would save like crazy and invest in all manner of things, from my own education to savings accounts and a pension. Now that I have a young niece and nephew and my own little girl, I am looking forward to the time when I can teach them all how to save and manage their money and I take great delight in buying them small silver coins (for birthdays and Christmas) along with tiny fractions of bitcoin, so that in the coming years (no matter how small it may be) they have something of *real* value. In my opinion, it is never too late to buy some bitcoin, especially if you believe that its value will grow for many years to come. Maybe the relatively small amount of bitcoin you buy won't mean you can retire early. It may not allow you to buy a new Ferrari next year or pay for an around the world cruise for your 50th birthday, but it might grow into a handsome kitty that you can put to good use. Or it might prove to be a nice little present for your own child and who knows, a few hundred pounds of bitcoin today could grow into a healthy deposit for *their* first home in the next decade or two. As an example of this, my father is looking to buy some bitcoin. Not looking for any financial gains for himself but to pass on to his granddaughter. He understands that this technology is young (and could come to nothing) but also understands that in the future, it could become widely adopted and be priced much higher. A few hundred pounds kept in fiat currency for a generation will likely end up being worth much less than the initial amount. Unless the owner can manage it extremely well and earn a good interest rate, however, the days of decent interest rates are behind us. Unfortunately, most of us will never experience great interest rates again, as negative interest rates are becoming the new normal. But transfer that fiat today into a rare commodity like gold or bitcoin and you *could* see that value rise multiple times (not financial advice).

I appreciate saving is seen as a personal *and* grown-up topic, along with one that is almost impossible for many people these days. Especially when our currency is so devalued and the cost of everyday items are ever-increasing. I shall get off my high horse now and hope that if nothing else, I have made a few readers think about how they could put a percentage of their disposable income to better use. Do not freeze with fear or inaction. Try to set in motion now, a couple of measures that mean you can do something positive with some of your 'spare' cash. Whether that's buying bitcoin or just saving fiat currency, act now and make your future that little bit brighter. At the end of this book in my chapter on further education, I reference a famous book originally printed in 1926 *'The Richest Man in Babylon'* by George S. Clason. I highly recommend this book for anyone interested in learning how to take control of their finances. The book gives financial advice through a collection of parables set 8,000 years ago in ancient Babylon. Reading the book, you will learn The Seven Cures for a Lean Purse and the Five Laws of Gold. To tickle your fancy, I shall give you the first cure for a lean purse: Start thy purse to fattening. The book's character Arkad, advises that we should save 10% of our income to start building up our wealth (the fattening of our purse). Arkad says "For every ten coins thou placest in your purse take out for use but nine. Thy purse will start to fatten at once and its increasing weight will feel good in thy hand and bring satisfaction to thy soul".

THE BITCOIN STANDARD

In a rather strange move for an author and his book, I would like to dedicate this chapter to a fellow Bitcoin author and his book. Whether Bitcoin 'succeeds' or not will be up for debate for many years to come, depending on how much adoption we see along with many other metrics. However, there is one thing I am sure of and that is that academics will be studying Bitcoin for many decades to come. There are already many who have made Bitcoin or cryptocurrency their life's work and I am certain we have only just scratched the surface.

From cryptographers, developers, and mathematicians through to finance professionals and economists, Bitcoin will keep many individuals and institutions busy for the foreseeable future.

One economist who has turned his sights towards Bitcoin is Dr Saifedean Ammous. He is from the Austrian school of the economic divide. Bitcoiners, gold bugs and libertarians see the Austrian economists as the enlightened Jedi knights of the economic world, with Keynesian economists fulfilling the role of the Sith Lords, with their strict and imperial or establishment orientated views. Many 'Austrian thinkers' believe that the Keynesian theories on economics have helped to put us in the financially sticky position we find ourselves in today.[11] Austrian economists believe a return to a sound monetary system along with a free market (instead of bureaucratically enforced markets) is the only way for humanity to financially evolve out of the debt-based mess we are in. The Austrians love of sound money is what makes their theories align with gold and silver

---

[11] Central banking, the abolishment of the Gold Standard and rampant money printing have all happened while governments followed Keynesian economics (those three points themselves are not necessarily Keynesian, but the economic standard which has been favoured by the world's largest governments over the last hundred years *has* been Keynesian).

investors and now the new generation of sound money advocates, the Bitcoiners.

Saifedean Ammous was an associate professor of economics at the Lebanese American University and a member of the Centre on Capitalism and Society at Columbia University. His book, *The Bitcoin Standard: The Decentralized Alternative to Central Banking* has been happily received by the Bitcoin community and will undoubtedly be read by many people who are new to the topic and wanting to learn about Bitcoin. To finish this part of the book we will briefly cover a few of the topics that Dr Ammous raises in his book.

<u>Hard Money</u>

Saifedean describes hard money as simply being money, which is hard to make. Gold is the hardest money humans have ever had. It is hard and costly to find and costly to refine. Money has historically always had the same qualities, these include things like its general acceptability, being divisible, durable, portable, stable, and fungible (meaning one unit is interchangeable and no different to any other unit). Austrians will also argue that another quality is that it should be hard to produce and arguably even harder to fake. If money is easy to produce then it can be manipulated by the people who control its manufacture. Logic would also suggest if it is easy and cheap to make, it should not be that valuable unless of course, a government enforces its value with a big stick. In his book, he describes the story of the West Africans and their monetary system of glass beads from around three hundred years ago. To the Africans, producing glass beads was both time consuming and costly, therefore the beads served quite well as hard money. However, all this changed once the Westerners arrived and twigged what the natives used as money. On their return to Europe, they set their factories into overdrive, cheaply making glass beads on an industrial scale and at a fraction of the cost.

They loaded their boats with the tiny beads, and on docking back in Africa were able to slowly buy up the real wealth of the land. Before the Africans had a chance to work out what was happening the damage had been done. The imported beads had such a negative effect on the Africans that they were ultimately renamed slave beads, as the glass beads were not only used to buy up large swathes of the country and its natural resources, but also human slaves. This one lesson from history is a good example to show that the harder the money is the better. The Africans were unlucky to meet the Westerners at that time. Another hundred years or so and they may have started to adopt gold, a much harder money compared to beads.

Stock-to-flow ratio

This is an interesting ratio and it shows the relationship between the current stockpile of a commodity (the stock) and the rate at which it is annually produced (the flow). Gold has the best stock-to-flow (S2F) ratio of any commodity on the planet. The two primary reasons for this is that it has been mined by humans for thousands of years and secondly, that it doesn't tarnish or rust away. This means that every ounce that humanity has *ever* mined is *still* available, still countable in the stock part of the equation, and therefore no matter how much humans try to mine it today, we can't inflate the overall supply massively because so much exists above ground. The flow side of the equation has also remained consistent because it has always been difficult to mine gold. Even today with larger machinery and better techniques, the flow is still comparatively low as the easy pickings have already been found by humans now long buried. We must dig deeper and deeper to uncover the remaining veins of gold. The S2F ratio of gold is currently 62:1. One way to visualise this figure is that it would take 62 years of mining gold (at our current capabilities) to mine the entire global stockpile. All of humanities' production, thousands of years of sourcing, mining, and refining could now be acquired in 62 years. This ratio is what makes gold the ultimate hard money. When other commodities are tested we see they have a much lower ratio, meaning it would take far less work to produce the entire supply and therefore they are less suited to be used as hard money. Palladium production can be matched in just over one year while Copper, Platinum, Wheat and Crude Oil all in less than one year. When Bitcoin is examined we see that it scores very well with a ratio of 50:1 and in the coming years, the bitcoin S2F ratio will outperform that of gold, thanks to the way the supply issuance is cut in half every four years. These halvings will play a big role in Bitcoin's S2F ratio and its price. Saifedean argues that already, bitcoin *is* good hard money and in a few short years, it will replace gold as the world's number one hard money. After the 2024 halving, it will reach 100:1 and from that point forward, we are in unexplored territory, as for the first time in history a commodity other than gold will hold the number one spot with regards to S2F.

Not only is bitcoin's supply reducing, but there is also a hard cap to the overall supply. Much more gold is available to us, we are just unable to currently access it. For example, our technological limitations prevent us from mining the vast seabeds where gold must be abundant, let alone all the countless tons of gold available to us in our solar system and the wider universe. Mining in space will affect golds S2F ratio, as will a heavily encrusted gold meteor crashing on earth. Bitcoin, however, cannot be overinflated and no matter how much work humanity push toward the goal, no more bitcoin can be created than the predetermined amount the software allows for. Regardless of the money (hardware and electricity) pumped into bitcoin production, only a set amount can be produced every day and once the 21 million cap is reached no more can be created.

Time Preference

The shorter your time preference, the happier you are to delay gratification. As we are talking finance here, it makes sense for us to think of this subject in relation to money. Simply put, if you have a short time preference you will likely want to save for the future, be that yours' or your children's, while if your time preference is long you will spend your money quickly and tend not to dwell on the long term implications of your spending and lack of saving. Saifedean describes that in many cases, the hardness of your money supply dictates what your time preference will be. If you live in a country with soft money (money that is cheap to make and that loses value over time), your time preference will be long and you will be forced to spend your government currency quickly before it is devalued. Conversely, when an individual uses hard money, such as when the world was on the Gold Standard, people saved their gold/money and looked to the future. Their time preference was now short, and they were able to delay personal gratification. Many were able to invest, invent, build businesses, save for their children's and grandchildren's future. He believes that humanity only truly flourishes when people can extend gratification beyond their lifetime and save wealth and build for future generations. He writes that over history you can tell when humanity has used soft and hard money and can witness the associated innovation and development that came with these times. According to his book, one of the most innovative times in recent human history was the 19th century. In this period many of the modern inventions we use today were invented and developed. We think many of these to be 20th-century inventions, but that's when these inventions were normalised, mass-marketed and produced globally. No, these were invented in the 1800s when the world was still on the Gold Standard. Remove the Gold Standard and by and large, society's time preference has flipped and now there is no delayed gratification.

Everything is wanted immediately, instant gratification. Fast food, fast next day delivery of our cheap and cheerful consumer goods and flat packed fast to assemble furniture. No savings, no personal pension plan, just an uncertain future where 'money' has no value and no methodical planning for the future is made. Thankfully our great grandparents lived in a world where gold ruled supreme and they collectively were able to invent the steam engine, the telephone, television, cement, locomotives, the internal combustion engine, the typewriter, antiseptics, anaesthesia, pasteurisation, moving pictures (film) and the electric light bulb, with the aeroplane missing out by only three years if you believe the Wright brothers invented powered flight and just eight years if you think it was invented by the Brazilian, Alberto Dumont.

I haven't done any real justice to Saifedeans book in this quick summary of a few good points he raises, and I hope that if reading my book sparks an interest, in either economics and/or Bitcoin you will consider reading *The Bitcoin Standard*. He theorises that in the future the central banks of the world could adopt Bitcoin as a means of final settlement, instead of them settling by transferring large amounts of currency and sometimes even gold between themselves. However, he has also stated that central bank adoption is unlikely as it means they will lose their control over the world. One interesting point he does make is that Bitcoin is possibly here to stay now and like the internet and many other technologies it cannot be eradicated or shut down. He believes the only way world governments could now crush Bitcoin would be to return to the Gold Standard. To improve the current system so much so that a technology and payment system like Bitcoin is simply not needed. Re-adopting gold and drastically improving global finances and fiscal policies could be the only measure they could take to stop the adoption of the hardest money humanity is likely to ever see.

One final point that he raises that is also interesting, is the concept that money has always been a technology. In my book, I use the term *store of value* quite a lot in reference to what Bitcoin is currently being used for. This means to use a commodity like gold or fine art or bitcoin to hold value for the long term. Incidentally, you may like to know that the rich do not use fiat currency to store much of their wealth, as they know that fiat loses value over time. That is why wealthy individuals utilise the stock market and other investment tools, such as property, land, jewellery, or gold, to try to preserve or even increase their capital. Saifedean raises the concept that bitcoin and other hard monies are a tool, a tool that is used to store value over the long term. He says that bitcoin or hard money in general, allows humans to store the fruits of their labour over time. This is an interesting concept that should be taught to all youngsters and could rejuvenate the concept of saving. The thought that you can save your physical labour (the sweat off your brow) today, encapsulate that labour in a technology that is resistant to erosion and government debasement and unpack it in the future is a very inspiring idea. If Bitcoin survives another decade and truly embeds itself into our society, it will be interesting to see Millennials and Gen Zs learn this concept and start saving for their future like many people from my generation were unable to do with a soft and worthless fiat currency.

Now you have learnt some of the basics, you can hang up your beginner's White Belt and I can award you with your very own Bitcoin Orange Belt. Due to your keen interest and ability to learn quickly, you have leapfrogged the Yellow Belt, well done! In the martial arts world, orange signifies the strengthening and the warming of the sun as it begins to prepare for all the new growth of the spring season. It also happens to be the main colour within the Bitcoin logo. Now we can move onto part two of this book, where we will learn some of the technical aspects of how Bitcoin works. I'm not going to lie to you, it may be a little confusing at times, but it will be required reading if you want to progress to become a Bitcoin Black Belt. I hope that I have written it in such a way that you easily understand it and find it enjoyable to read. Remember that just because it is technical you shouldn't be put off by it. The internet is extremely technical; however, we are all capable of using it without understanding all, or any of the various systems and protocols that allow the internet as we know it to work. If we know how to plug in the router, set a secure password and click a few buttons on our computer or phone to connect, we are up and running, Bitcoin is no different. A healthy, safe, and basic understanding of how it works is desirable, but we don't need to know how every facet works in detail. Let's leave that to the computer scientists, cryptologists or the individuals who have an aptitude for this stuff and wish to dig deeper. As I included some quotes from the ageing and failing legacy system earlier, let's now finish this part of the book with some modern quotes from the new economy. From supporters, entrepreneurs and business people involved in this new sector.

"I do think Bitcoin is the first encrypted money that has the potential to do something like change the world".
- Peter Thiel, Co-founder PayPal.

"Every informed person needs to know about Bitcoin because it might be one of the world's most important developments".
- Leon Luow, Nobel peace prize nominee.

"Bitcoin was created to serve a highly political intent, a free and uncensored network where all can participate with equal access".
- Amir Taaki, Anarchist, Programmer and Hacktivist.

"When I first heard about Bitcoin, I thought it was impossible. How can you have a purely digital currency? Can't I just copy your hard drive and have your bitcoins? I didn't understand how that could be done, and then I looked into it and it was brilliant".

-Jeff Garzik, Former Bitcoin code developer, engineer and entrepreneur.

"Bitcoin is the currency of resistance".

- Max Keiser, Broadcaster.

"There are only going to be 21 million coins, there are billions of people in the world, some reasonable percentage of who might find it interesting to own a piece of Bitcoin".

-Adam Back, Original cypherpunk, businessman and cryptographer.

PART II

THE TECHIE SCIENCE BIT

M y deep technical understanding of Bitcoin is limited. Therefore, I shall only explain the basics, knowing that most readers will be put off by all the mathematical and scientific processes that enable it to work. I believe that most people these days (those who are not engineers or techies at least) are not interested in the various intricacies of how some technologies work. I believe that many people only want to know the high-level information at best. Then, if an interest is sparked, they may wish to investigate the inner workings further. As an example, I imagine that not many people know or understand the many intricate protocols that are used behind the scenes by your high street bank when you use your contactless debit card. However, I am sure that every reader knows how to use their card, they just don't know (and don't care to know) how the technology allows it to work. For most people, this thinking will be consistent through all technologies, from your bank card and the internet to your microwave oven and even that automatic toothpick dispenser you've been looking at buying.

Although I have tried to write this as easily as I can for newcomers you should not be disheartened if you find it hard or impossible to grasp. As I said above, not everyone is built that way and at the end of the day, a basic understanding is all that is needed. This book will give you the basics, but feel free to dig deeper if you wish to learn more on any individual subject covered. I believe the average person should aim to learn much more after reading this book. Also, learning from multiple perspectives is not a bad thing at all, especially when it relates to complicated and technical information such as this and something so crucial as personal finance.

In this section of the book, we will look at the following aspects of Bitcoin:

- Cryptography.

- Blockchain (the new technology that records all the transactions).

- Bitcoin addresses (Where bitcoin are stored).

- How these addresses are made.

- Bitcoin keys.

- Transaction confirmations.

- Wallets (programs we use to send and receive our bitcoin).

- How 'bitcoins' are made (aka bitcoin mining).

- How people can use the Bitcoin code to make their own cryptocurrency.

These concepts may seem quite alien to begin with, but if you hold on you will slowly see that there isn't too much to fear. In-Depth knowledge of these subjects will not be critical to a newcomer; however, it is fair to say that an understanding of many of these points will make things much easier for you in the long run. You will have a greater appreciation of the technology and a good understanding of how it works. You will also be safer than most new people entering the space *and* be able to explain how it works to family and friends who show an interest.

CRYPTOGRAPHY

B itcoin is based around cryptography. Cryptography is the practice and study of securing communications in the presence of third parties, known as adversaries. Said more simply, it allows us to protect messages from snooping eyes. For our purpose, cryptography at its most basic level revolves around encryption and decryption. Encryption is the method of turning a readable message into unreadable text, which is then referred to as ciphertext. Conversely, decryption is turning that unreadable ciphertext back into your original legible message. It enables information to be safely scrambled and then reconstructed by the recipient, meaning it is a secure way of communicating between people. Encryption has been used in varying degrees for centuries. Early signs of its use go back to Greek and even Egyptian times. A famous tool once used by the Spartans was called a scytale, which is a simple wooden baton or cylinder. A long strip of leather was coiled around and down the scytale. The user would write their message down the leather on one axis. Uncoiling the strip would now reveal the message broken up by large spaces (due to it being coiled around the baton). These spaces were then filled in with random letters, turning the message into unreadable ciphertext. Then the message could be stored or transported via messenger to its destination. On arrival, the recipient would have to recoil it on their scytale (which would need to have the same diameter) to be able to read the original message. Not a foolproof use of encryption, but it was clever enough until everyone knew of its use.

In more recent history, encryption was the technology used by the famous German Enigma cypher machines used during the Second World War. These machines played a big role for the Nazi war machine by encrypting all military communications. From the Panzer tank divisions movements and Luftwaffe sorties, to a slightly more complex model handling all top military and U-boat communications. Eventually, it was cracked by the mathematician and cryptanalyst Alan Turing and his team of code-breakers at Bletchley Park, England (portrayed in the 2015 film *The Imitation Game*). Cracking the Enigma machine was no mean feat, as it took a vast amount of ingenuity and the creation of one of the world's first computers to do so. Historians believe it shortened the war in Europe by as much as two years and saved up to fourteen million lives! Today's computers are worlds apart from Turing's analogue computer. The latest smartphones, for example, have a million times more RAM than the flight computers used during the Apollo space missions! With modern techniques and faster, more powerful computers, basic encryption has transformed from its beginnings. Today cryptography is used to securely handle all manner of electronic communications and data transfer and is used extensively by the military, along with technologies such as email, social media, personal banking and now the future of finance...cryptocurrency.

Bitcoin is the world's first cryptocurrency! It has taken the science of cryptography and produced a payment network that is safe and allows us to financially interact together by ourselves. How does Bitcoin use cryptography? We will look at this in the coming pages but simply put for now, we can say that a Bitcoin address (the term for our cryptocurrency account number) is created using cryptography. The database (or 'spreadsheet') that records all the bitcoin transactions, which is called a blockchain, also uses cryptography to secure the data. As you will see throughout this book, blockchains are just as revolutionary as cryptocurrency.

BLOCKCHAIN

Satoshi Nakamoto gave us Bitcoin and at the same time, she gave us another new technology called a blockchain. It is the blockchain which we can visualise as being like a large 'spreadsheet/digital accounts book'. The American name for an accounts book is a ledger, so some people call blockchain technology, ledger technology. Either way regardless of the name you use, blockchains are a fundamental part of nearly all cryptocurrencies.

The Bitcoin blockchain holds (among other things) all the transactional data performed on the network. Anyone can view the blockchain and see the transactions that have happened. It is this blockchain, that is spread around the world on many nodes (computers) making it distributed. Hence another name that is used to describe blockchain: Distributed Ledger Technology or DLT. When someone sends bitcoin to another person, the network of nodes that are running the Bitcoin code, will automatically check with the blockchain (the digital accounts book) to make sure it is a valid transaction. If it is valid, once processed, *all* the copies of the blockchain are automatically updated, therefore we don't require banks to help us; blockchains allow us to do it ourselves.

Every time bitcoin are sent, the transaction is recorded on the blockchain so that everyone can see and prove that the transaction took place, at what time and which addresses (accounts) were involved. Our high street banks also record all our fiat transactions, but they alone hold this data and they alone store it on their private and centralised servers. This privacy, which is understood from one perspective, can also lead to deceitful and even illegal behaviour.

It allows, among other things, for some banks to launder criminal currency and for some governments to embezzle funds. All this secrecy helps to hide these acts and is one reason why there is so much distrust of banks and government's financial spending today. Distrust is never going to disappear in the traditional system, but these malicious actions can cause mass instability and in worst cases recessions or even depressions. However, in Bitcoin, as we shall learn shortly, deceitful behaviour is not allowed. The computer code that manages the Bitcoin network will not allow participants to bend or break the rules.

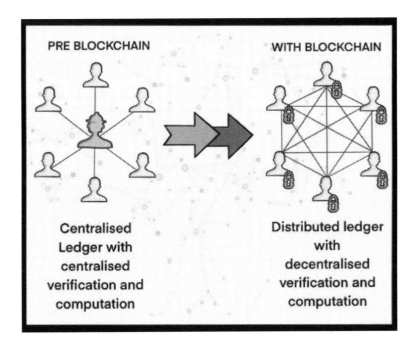

The Bitcoin blockchain stores three things

- The transaction history.
- The addresses where the bitcoin are stored.
- The bitcoin themselves.

Transaction History

The Bitcoin blockchain records all the transactions into chunks of data, called blocks. A new block is created (roughly) every ten minutes. This block is then cryptographically attached to the previous block, creating a chain of blocks, hence the name blockchain. We can all publicly view the blockchain and verify a transaction. We can also all agree that the blockchain is up-to-date and that it hasn't been altered (due to the highly technical way the blockchain works, as it would take lots of computing power to attack and alter the Bitcoin blockchain, and to date it has never happened).

Storing our bitcoin on the blockchain

As we know, bitcoin are digital, no physical coins or notes exist. But it gets a little more complicated. All the bitcoin that currently exist, live on the blockchain and not on user's computers or smartphones, although that is how it appears. In part one, and up until this point I have implied that the coins live on our devices, this is not the case. This was not to mislead you, but just for ease of understanding, while you were learning some of the basics. bitcoin reside on the blockchain.

The bitcoin, the addresses (accounts) and the transactional data *all* reside on the blockchain. Now I must admit it gets one level more confusing than that, now brace yourself...'bitcoins' do not actually exist! That's right, there is no such thing as even a digital bitcoin. When you 'own' a bitcoin, or a fraction of a bitcoin, all you really own is the balance of it, or if you like, the receipt that you own it. The bitcoin resides in an address that you control/own so you *do* in fact own it, but physically and even digitally nothing really exists. You do not possess any digital file or 'thing' which *is* a bitcoin. (You *will*, however, have a file on your device, which holds important data which relates to the 'bitcoin' you own, but no physical/digital bitcoin itself).

When we transact bitcoin to one another, all that happens is that the blockchain updates the balance of each address involved in the transaction. There is no movement per se, just a change of balance. This is hopefully not too crazy to visualise, and in some respects, it is no different to how banks and large organisations manage our currency and our customer loyalty tokens, such as rewards points or air miles. Our cash, loyalty tokens and air miles are stored on centralised systems, and 'issued' accordingly, but are never actually moved, balances are just increased or decreased. Simply put balances are just adjusted and then recorded. Bitcoin operates in the same way, although it is decentralised, and everyone can view and agree on the state of the network at any time.

For an example of how bitcoin move, let's imagine I wanted to send you 0.003 of a bitcoin. The blockchain already knows that my address contains 0.004 bitcoin and let's say that your balance is 0.10000650 bitcoin. I would initiate the transfer; my wallet software transmits the request. Node operators will pass the request around the world to one another, and in turn, pass it to the Bitcoin Miners (who process the transactions and also create new coins). The miner's computers will check that the transaction is valid and if all is well, the transaction is processed, the blockchain is updated and my addresses balance is adjusted to 0.001 and 0.003 is added to your address, making your balance now 0.10300650. No bitcoin moved (as they don't exist) but the balances of both our wallets have changed accordingly. Remember that once the blockchain has been updated, all the nodes then hold the new updated version. This means everyone is on the same page and everyone knows the current state of the network and who owns what.

As you are starting to appreciate, Bitcoin is very technical, and I wasn't lying when I stated at the start of this book that most people would not be able to master many of the skill sets required to fully understand it on a deep level.

For a more thorough understanding of how bitcoin transactions work you will need to research inputs, outputs, UTXOs and change addresses. A UTXO stands for Unspent Transaction Output and is basically a technical name for each little 'part' or previously received transaction (or output as it is called) within our balance.

In many cases, our balance will be made up from lots of different, formally received transactions. These small chunks of bitcoin cannot be broken up once received. This is a little hard to explain and visualise but imagine that Alice sends me 0.5 bitcoin and straight away I wish to pay Bob 0.25 bitcoin. Because the UTXO I hold from Alice is 0.5 bitcoin, I must send it in its entirety to Bob. I cannot break it down into smaller chunks. I must send Bob the entire 0.5 BTC and in the process, 0.25 will go to him and 0.25 will automatically come back to me in the form of change. From my perspective I will only send him the required amount of 0.25, however, my wallet will not be able to deconstruct or break down my 0.5 UTXO from Alice and will send the full amount but in the process it will automatically create a second transaction back to me for the change, being the other 0.25 BTC. I hope those last few sentences have not blown too many minds. For those interested, and for a greater understanding of how transactions work, you can visit this website linked below. https://www.thebalance.com / how-does-a-bitcoin-transaction-work-391213

Other benefits of blockchains

Nobody knows *exactly* how many fiat pounds and dollars there are in circulation. As people stuff notes under their mattresses along with accidentally dropping pennies/cents down drains or collecting rare 50 pence pieces or dimes, hence an accurate figure would be impossible to work out. We are also unsure of how many more pounds and dollars are going to be printed in the future. But with Bitcoin's open source code, and its accompanying blockchain we know:

- How many are going to be mined and at what rate.
- How many are in existence right now and what addresses they are held in. This is why Satoshi designed Bitcoin and its blockchain; to return some order and trust to our economy.

As we can see, blockchains store transactional data, but they can also store other information. In the future, the Bitcoin blockchain (and other blockchains) *could* store all manner of data for us. Because of its strength against hacking and its immutability, (the inability to change data once inside the blockchain) we can all trust this technology to safely hold other sensitive data for us. Bitcoin is disrupting the financial world; it could also do the same to other sectors too. House ownership deeds, voting, birth certificates, supply chain management, medical records and personal wills are just a few examples of services that Bitcoin and/or other networks could disrupt for the better.

<u>Transaction Fees</u>

Bitcoin is not free to use. As we shall see later, large amounts of computing power and electricity are used to manage and secure the Bitcoin network. The fees help to pay for these costs and also incentivise people to help Bitcoin operate. The people who process the transactions are known as miners, and we shall look closely at them and their incentives in an upcoming chapter. One incentive for a miner is the transaction fees that they can earn. Fees are not static. They can change depending on the load being put on the system. Individual users can also adjust the fee they pay, depending on how quickly they want their transaction to be processed. On face value, it may be a little hard for a newcomer to stomach the idea of transaction fees, as these days our cash can be sent for free. This may be true in many cases, however, remember the banks profit from their customers in many other ways, from loans, mortgages and now even accounts that some people pay for monthly. Remember also, that international payments are not free, some organisations charge high percentage fees for the privilege. Virtually all cryptocurrencies charge a transaction fee to their users, and they generally cost anywhere from a few pennies to a pound or so. Bitcoin fees are generally the highest in the space, however, in late 2019 a user sent over 44,000 bitcoin in a single transaction, worth around £240 million at the time, and for only £0.25 in fees. We can only imagine what this would have cost in the traditional system. As we shall learn later, fees on the Bitcoin blockchain did increase massively in 2017 due to the high demand for transaction space. They have since normalised and as Bitcoin is continually improving, new technologies have been developed to reduce the fees even more.

KEYS

Keys are special, long numbers that our Bitcoin wallet (account) uses to manage our coins. They act as our 'digital keys' allowing us to 'unlock' our wallet and send/spend the bitcoin inside. The subject of Bitcoin keys is complicated to thoroughly explain, so I will aim to give you the basics, the main points that a beginner needs to know to safely use Bitcoin. There will be many Bitcoin users out there who do not know some of the following information. Do they know enough to keep themselves and their bitcoin safe? This is unknown; however, I hope to arm you with as much knowledge as I can to make sure you are an informed and safe user.

- Your Bitcoin wallet is a computer program that we use to view our balance, send and receive bitcoin. (We shall look at these in an upcoming chapter).

- When you open a wallet for the very first time, it generates you a very long, random number. This number is called your private key.

- This private key is then used to produce two more long random numbers.

- One is called your public key.

- The other is your Bitcoin address. This is where your bitcoin are stored and can be best visualised as a location on the blockchain.

- These three numbers are cryptographically related to one another.

Note: Modern wallets have a very handy and user-friendly backup feature. For this reason, you should not be too alarmed by what you read in this chapter. Our keys are extremely important, but just because we have a very clever way of backing them up and restoring them, it does not mean we should be reckless with them.

Your public key (as the name suggests) can be shared with people publicly and your private key, yes you've guessed it, should be kept private! Key management is handled automatically by your wallet software, so users do not need to do anything with these keys to send or receive bitcoin. The keys themselves are located deep within the files of your wallet's application folder. Your only task is to keep your private key safe, along with any associated backup passwords or something called a seed phrase which we shall look at in the chapter on wallets. Your third number is your Bitcoin address, this is what we use to receive bitcoin. It is the address (location) on the blockchain that you control (by having the associated public/private key pair). This Bitcoin address is what we share with people to allow them to send bitcoin to us. We share our email address with people to receive emails and now in the cryptocurrency age, we share our Bitcoin address to receive bitcoin. We will look a little closer at addresses in the next chapter.

Simply put, your private and public keys are used to encrypt and decrypt your bitcoin transactions. The private key encrypts the transaction, while your public key is used by the recipient to decrypt the transaction once they receive it. That's the science of what your keys are doing in two simple sentences, however, we need to learn how important it is to protect your private key. Your private key is what controls your access/ability to spend the funds in your wallet. Lose your private key and you have lost all access to your bitcoin (until you use your handy restore function that is). However, just because you can easily restore your private key and reclaim access to your bitcoin you should not become complacent! Keeping your private key secure and in your control is important, especially when you learn that an individual with your private key can 'sweep' your Bitcoin address empty in a matter of seconds. So yes, they are extremely important! For this reason, you could almost argue that your private key *is* your bitcoin, that's how important it is.

One meme to spread throughout the Bitcoin community was the phrase, 'not your keys not your bitcoin'. This meme highlighted the importance of owning and securing your private keys yourself, for individuals to hold their own bitcoin and not to rely on exchanges or third-party custodians to protect these digital assets. Hopefully by the time you have finished this chapter that meme will make sense. Within the traditional monetary system, your Bitcoin private key is comparable to the key to the bank's vault. Not only that, but it is also the keys to the forklift and armoured truck needed to transfer all the currency and gold out of the bank. Private keys are your digital identification, your digital proof of ownership and without the private key, you are locked out of the wallet. As mentioned above, your keys are safely stored in a file in your wallet's application folder on your hard drive (in the case of using a PC or phone wallet) and must remain in their folder for you to be able to use the wallet. If you move that specific file from its folder, your wallet will not be able to sync with the Bitcoin blockchain and therefore not be able to show you your balance or let you use your bitcoin. However, if you then returned that file back to its home (original location), your wallet *would* be able to sync with the blockchain and your balance and access to your bitcoin would be restored. Should you one day be tidying up your hard drive to make some additional space and purposefully or accidentally, delete the wallet's folder you will have deleted all possible chance of accessing those coins. That is until you use the clever restore function I keep mentioning. Although, just because this restore function is available you should not become blasé with your Bitcoin security.

As you can see, your private key is important and very valuable, so you do not want to lose it or let it fall into the wrong hands. For this reason, you should not go searching for your private key (thinking you are being clever) and copy and paste it into an email to yourself. Do not send it to 'the cloud' such as a service like Dropbox believing you are storing them safely there. Your email inbox, Dropbox and the Apple iCloud are *not* secure! Do not send them to someone who is trying to provide you with tech support and claims that they need it. This is yours and yours only! We will cover wallets and the clever backup feature that they use shortly, so please do not be put off by this technical information. I just felt that I needed to detail how important private keys are and what they are used for. Also, it is relevant to note that the newest generation of wallets (known as hardware wallets) are so secure, users can't even accidentally delete or lose the private key.

Understanding keys and their importance is probably one of the hardest things within this book, so now that we have discussed them you can sit back and enjoy what remains, knowing the hardest part is most likely behind you. Go and pop the kettle on or pour yourself a small cocktail to celebrate. Only have the one cocktail though, as there are still a few tricky concepts to learn in this part of the book.

BITCOIN ADDRESS

Your Bitcoin address is used to receive bitcoin and is the physical location on the blockchain where they are stored. It was made for you by your wallet software when you first opened the wallet. It is made from your private key and is cryptographically linked to both your public and private keys. You *can* publicly share it with people to allow them to send bitcoin to your wallet. No trust is needed when sharing your Bitcoin address with people, as in having your Bitcoin address people can only send you coins; they cannot remove them from your wallet, as to remove bitcoin from your wallet they would need… that's right your private key.

You could, if you wanted, post your Bitcoin address onto a Facebook or forum page for the whole world to see. Although this would not be great Op-Sec (operational security) as the general public would then be able to see the balance of your address and follow your bitcoin and subsequent spending/sending of these bitcoin on the blockchain. It would be far safer to send individual people a different address to send you bitcoin. Then unless everyone colluded, nobody would know how much bitcoin you had, as at best each person could only ever search the balance of the address you had given them.

A Bitcoin address is 26-35 characters long. They are alphanumeric.[12] A Bitcoin address can also be represented as a QR code, as seen on the following page. Once you have your first Bitcoin wallet and if you wanted the practice, I would be honoured if your first transaction was a tip to me to help

---

[12] Made of numbers and letters. They also include upper and lowercase letters. Original Bitcoin addresses start with the digit 1, whereas the newer generations start with a 3 or bc1. To help reduce confusion they will not include a capital 'O' and '0' as well as capital 'I' and lower-case 'l'.

support my mission. You can scan my QR code with your smartphone or webcam and it will automatically translate the QR code into *my* Bitcoin address and even input my address into the 'send to' field within your wallet ready to use. Alternatively, you can type out my address manually. You will notice that my Bitcoin address begins with the digit 3 which means it is a multisig address. This is an extra secure type of address, where more than one person has a private key to the same address. We discuss multisig addresses a little more in the security chapter, but simply put for now they require more than one person to sign a transaction, making them a suitable way for a person or business to increase their security. This is the Bitcoin address for this book:

3P4vJM7yVBiPnZh7cDYVqXjxkMFTarb

It is not essential, but Bitcoin addresses are designed and recommended for a one time, single-use. We should not reuse the same address repeatedly. Some people would strongly argue that we should *never* reuse it. This may seem strange, as in the traditional banking world we only have one account number and we reuse it all the time, sharing it with everyone. However, in the new economy, each time you wish to receive bitcoin, you should generate a brand new Bitcoin address. This may seem crazy, but it is done for security reasons and it will ultimately help to shield your identity from any Bitcoin addresses you control. This sentence should not scare anyone, but as we know, hackers and thieves will for evermore be monitoring all cryptocurrency blockchains. If you reuse addresses and depending on how blasé you were, such as linking it to websites, forums or handing them out to colleagues and friends, slowly but surely you will be leaving a trail of digital breadcrumbs of this address and its use, which could be followed back to you if a hacker, thief, company, blockchain analysis firm, or government agency chose to thoroughly investigate. To avoid any chance of a digital trail forming in the first place, users who care for their security or anonymity will generate new Bitcoin addresses and discard them after just *one* use. You will find that all wallets will generate you a new receiving address very easily and it will be very clear on how to do this. Remember that it costs nothing to generate a new Bitcoin address, so if it can increase your privacy and security, why would you not use a new address whenever possible?

Here's the real mind-boggling part about generating new addresses. If millions or even one day billions of users are generating hundreds or even thousands of addresses at random and as required (every time they wish to receive a new transaction), what is the likelihood that we will run out of potential Bitcoin addresses? Also, we know that Bitcoin addresses are randomly generated, so how likely is it that someone will generate an already existing address (one that is already in use)? Because there are so many characters in a Bitcoin address (up to 35 alpha-numeric characters) the actual number of possible Bitcoin addresses is unbelievably huge. According to my research it is a massive 1,461,501,637,330,902, 918,203,684,832,716,283,019,655,932,542,976 addresses! A pretty big number I'm sure you'll agree. To put that number into perspective there are an estimated 7 Quintillion grains of sand on the planet, which is a drop in the ocean compared to the number of potential Bitcoin addresses. One quintillion has 18 zeros! So, as you can see the above number of possible Bitcoin addresses is very large (with its 48 zeros).

So, we can all individually generate thousands of addresses, happy in the knowledge that they'll never be any remote chance that anyone will generate an already existing Bitcoin address (so long as the wallet software uses a safe and trusted means to randomly generate these addresses). Private key generation is also just as safe. One way to describe how unlikely it would be for a private key to be generated twice, is that if a million people could generate a million private keys every second, it would still take billions and billions of years before two identical keys were produced!

BITCOIN WALLETS

As we have already learnt, a Bitcoin wallet is where we 'store' our digital assets/coins. Or more accurately, where we view our blockchain balance. Think of it as your bank account, or more accurately your crypto bank, as once we enter the new economy we effectively become our own bank. They can be wallets that you control from your PC or mobile phone, or small electronic devices called hardware wallets. You can also have a wallet with an online cryptocurrency exchange.
A cryptocurrency wallet allows you to send and receive crypto. Some will be tailor-made for one specific cryptocurrency, while others can hold multiple different cryptos at the same time.
A Bitcoin wallet can have lots of separate Bitcoin addresses within it, this makes it easy for you to see all your different balances at the same time. You may want one address to store bitcoin for everyday spending. Another address could be where you plan to keep bitcoin for future use, with another separate address being used for your upcoming holiday or car purchase etc. Virtually all the wallets that we use today are known as HD wallets, which stands for hierarchical deterministic. This relates to the way your keys are randomly generated by the wallet software. Before we look at the various types of wallets available we shall look at how HD wallets are backed up (protected).

When you open a Bitcoin HD wallet for the first time, there is a setup process that you will have to go through. The software will ask you to have a pen or pencil and a piece of paper to hand while doing this. Depending on the wallet software it will present you with either 12, 18 or 24 random words. Collectively these are known as your seed phrase, seed recovery phrase or backup seed phrase. These 'wallet words' are what you will have to jot down onto your piece of paper. Once you have checked that these words have been written down correctly you are all set. This seed phrase is all you need should you get locked out of your wallet for any reason. Should your PC break, or you accidentally delete your private key, you are protected by having these words safely stored. Your seed phrase *is* your Bitcoin private key, converted into word form, how cool is that. We have the science to turn a long random string of numbers and letters into readable English words.

Another point to note is that you should *not* photograph, or screen shoot your seed phrase, as you do not want a digital copy to exist *anywhere* on your phone, hard drive or cloud that a hacker could potentially access! Just like we learnt earlier with your private key, no unnecessary digital duplicating of this seed phrase should be undertaken. After all, this seed phrase *is* your private key in word form! *No* scanning it into your computer or emailing it to yourself, no digital copies should be made anywhere full stop, your backup seed phrase should only ever be handwritten. I'll repeat that sentence just one more time to make sure this is clear. **No digital copy of your seed recovery phrase should ever be made. It should only ever be handwritten.** Your task now is to protect that piece of paper. According to the Wikipedia page on seed phrases, using a pencil is a safer option to a pen (as it is less likely to fade). It also suggests using acid-free or even archival paper and then storing it in the dark, avoiding extremes of heat and moisture. In my opinion specialist paper is not a necessity for a newcomer, but for a person who is holding a serious amount of bitcoin and/or for long term storage, the Wikipedia advice is good. They also suggest that tearing the paper into two pieces and storing them in separate locations is a bad idea, as if one half is found then an attacker can brute force (make multiple guesses) the missing words a lot easier. Many individuals will use a safe deposit box or the services of their solicitor/custody agent to help keep these safe, again especially if large amounts of bitcoin are at stake. However, I'm sure most people just keep theirs in a safe place at their home. If you search the internet you will see the many ways people are storing their seed phrase, from writing their own encryption programs, writing the words separately in seemingly random places or just using an old notebook. With some even whisking the words off to a relative in a different part of the country or even a different continent. There are even special stainless steel devices that enable you to protect your seed phrase. Using such a device can give great peace of mind, as you know that your backup is now safe from water and fire damage, along with fading and staining. One such product is called the Capsule, from the company Cryptosteel. This device (which is around the size of a marker pen) safely stores your seed phrase, letter by letter, on small steel tiles, which you load into the metal device, which are then securely protected inside by a tough steel cylindrical outer sheath. The device is fireproof up to 1,400C and will protect your important seed phrase for a lifetime. Visit my website to see a demo video and as with all the items I strongly recommend in this book, I would be tickled pink that if you fancy getting your hands on one, you followed my referral link https://cryptosteel.com/product/cryptosteel-capsule/?csr=565 As I have stressed more than once now, please be very careful with these words. If you try to be clever on how you hide or disguise them and then forget how to find or unite them, you will have put yourself in a sticky position, having put your access to your bitcoin at risk. A fitting and famous saying from the computer security sector is 'complexity is the enemy of security'. For this reason, most people will simply write them down on paper and protect their seed phrase sensibly. For those serious Bitcoiners, a Capsule from Cryptosteel is a must buy and will protect your seed phrase and bitcoin for life.

Should your phone or PC break or get stolen, all you will need to do (having got a new device and reloaded the wallet software) is to select 'Restore Wallet' and then input your seed phrase. This will effectively restore and open your old wallet for you. The wallet software will resync with the Bitcoin blockchain and your access to your funds will be restored. Again, this is why it is important to make sure you store your seed phrase in a safe place! Remember, when you enter the Bitcoin revolution you are effectively becoming your own bank and you are responsible for your security. There is no support number to call if you lose your recovery phrase! **The company that made the wallet software will not be able to help you in any way with any seed phrase recovery**, you are on your own (as these words are randomly generated). They are your words and nobody on the planet can find them for you. Please take serious note of this next sentence. **There is no 'renew' password button in Bitcoin. Once you enter the space and initiate your wallet you are 100% responsible for your security, your seed phrase, your private key...everything.** In almost all cases there is nothing anyone can do to assist you with lost passwords or lost seed phrases. Unfortunately, it is so easy these days for people to forget their passwords almost on purpose, knowing they can click the renew password button. Please remember that this is *not* an option in Bitcoin unless you use the service of a custodian, such as an exchange, but then you are not adhering to the meme 'not your keys not your bitcoin'.

Once you have a wallet and bitcoin stored in it, remember that the assets are never actually held in that wallet. Your bitcoin are stored on the Bitcoin blockchain. Your wallet is just a fancy program used for receiving bitcoin to your address on the blockchain, along with authorising the sending of them. It also stores your keys and shows you the balance of the associated addresses. So, the bitcoin reside on the Bitcoin blockchain. Your wallet will synchronize with the blockchain and check the addresses that you own (have private keys for) and show the balances of these addresses to you. Your wallet is, therefore, an interface with the blockchain. All cryptocurrencies 'live' on their respective blockchains! Therefore, you can conceivably lose or break your PC/phone/hardware wallet and having imported your seed phrase into a new wallet, restore access to your bitcoin. The funds were never actually lost, just the way of accessing and spending them was lost, ultimately your private key was lost. This is why protecting your private key/backup seed phrase is so important.

One last point to mention before we look at the different types of wallets available is the term hot and cold storage/wallets. These terms are used to describe how secure the means of storage is. A hot wallet is simply a Bitcoin wallet that is connected to the internet. This includes most Bitcoin wallets, from the wallets people have on their phones and PCs to exchange wallets, where people buy and sell cryptocurrency. These are the most common and to some extent, the most user-friendly and easily accessible wallets. Because they connect to the internet, hackers can potentially attack these remotely. These types of wallets are commonly used by hundreds of thousands of people daily and are safe enough for most people to use, as and when required, but a good habit to form would be to not hold too much bitcoin on them. An analogy with the regular, legacy banking system would be how we as individuals hold cash. We happily walk around with small amounts of cash on us all the time. In our homes, we may feel happy storing a little more. However, we wouldn't be particularly happy or confident if we were having to protect our life savings or pension in the same way. For a safer and more robust bitcoin storage solution, people and companies will hold most of their bitcoin holdings in what is called cold storage. Cold storage, or a cold wallet, means that the private keys do not touch the internet, so no direct use of computers or phones. In this situation, the private keys are stored on a device called a hardware wallet, or for advanced users, a computer that has never touched the internet (aka an air-gapped computer). There are pros and cons to using hot and cold wallets, but the general rule of thumb is, the greater the amount being secured, the colder the wallet should be. We will now look at the different wallets available to people.

Paper wallets: In the early days of Bitcoin, users could generate their own keys and print them off onto pieces of paper. Paper wallets looked quite stylish and resembled a cheque or bond to some extent. These were the first generation of cold wallets *if* created properly. However, they are now not seen as being particularly safe, due to it being quite difficult to make one securely. These wallets are not recommended for beginners and few people will make one these days unless they are extremely computer/security savvy.

Brain wallets: A brain wallet is where you memorise your seed phrase. Having memorised these words (and then bravely deleted the private key off your device) you can now travel the world happy in the knowledge that your bitcoin fortune 'travels' with you always. All you need to do, when you wish to gain access to your bitcoin, is to load a compatible wallet onto your computer/phone, input your seed phrase using the restore wallet function and voilà, your bitcoin wealth is accessible. Also not recommended for beginners and forgetful people as obviously you would kick yourself if you forgot your recovery phrase. Please note you should not delete your private key.

PC and phone wallets: Aka software wallets. These are 'hot wallets' as our devices obviously touch the internet. Wallet software has come a long way from the early days of Bitcoin, attempting to make the user experience and security easier for new people joining the community and there are many different ones available on the market. I cannot easily detail the functionality of a wallet, but as I said earlier they enable you to send and receive bitcoin as well as view your transactional history. Wallets act as an interface, between you and the Bitcoin blockchain. In many respects, they look like your banking app or PayPal account. To best understand how a Bitcoin wallet looks and behaves, a search on YouTube is all you need. According to an article on 99bitcoins which was updated in May 2020, the top five IOS wallets in order are, Ledger Nano X,

Edge, Abra, Green wallet and Coinomi. Their article on android wallets (updated in the same month) recommends (again in order), Ledger Nano X, Coinomi, Abra, Edge and the Atomic Wallet. Before you download any wallet software, please be sure to check that the wallet is still being recommended by multiple sources and there has been no bad press about it. This could be done via a simple internet search, including the wallets name plus the words + news, or + complaints. Another way of researching if a wallet or service is still operating safely would be a YouTube or Twitter search for any recent news, developments, or bad press. As with all software and companies, they can come and go, so it is the responsibility of the reader to check what is available and safe at the time they wish to download.

Hardware wallets: These small cold storage devices (which are small enough to sit in your palm) add an extra layer of security for cryptocurrency users. They are considerably more secure than the above-mentioned PC and phone wallets for reasons we shall quickly see. They connect to your PC or phone through a USB cable, with newer models also utilising Bluetooth. They are considered by most experts as the safest way to hold your bitcoin. The reason for this is that they stop your private key from ever touching your computer and therefore the internet (making it *extremely* hard for hackers to gain access to your private key and in turn your crypto). There is a little computer chip called a secure element inside the device (this is the same chip used on our bank cards). This chip allows us to safely transact without the private keys ever 'touching' the PC.
You can use these hardware devices on untrusted and even virus-infected machines, as the secure element creates a barrier between the PC and your important private key.

Setup will be the same as detailed above, with an HD recovery seed phrase. Once your device is connected to your PC/phone, the hardware wallet is unlocked with a four-digit PIN that you set and then it behaves no differently to a regular PC Bitcoin wallet. Hardware wallets usually operate via the hardware wallet companies' app so users will need this program installed on their PC/phone to use these wallets. Should you lose the device, it breaks, gets stolen, don't panic. A new hardware wallet (or even just a compatible PC wallet) and your seed phrase are all you need to restore your wallet and regain access to your crypto! There are a few hardware wallets available on the market with more appearing as time goes on. Keepkey, Trezor and Ledger are the original hardware wallet providers, with Coldcard being a new arrival. In Appendix C I have detailed a few security considerations a person using a hardware wallet may want to be aware of. Especially the steps you should quickly take if your hardware wallet is stolen. So, jumping back to the analogy of not wanting to carry your life savings on you all the time in cash form, many people in the crypto space will utilise a hardware wallet for the same reason. You might use a PC/phone 'hot' wallet to hold the bitcoin you intend to use daily, your cash so to speak, and a hardware 'cold' wallet for your longer-term holdings and savings.

Exchange wallets: (The place where we buy bitcoin). When you open an account with an exchange you will automatically receive a wallet as part of your account. You can hold, send and receive your crypto in this wallet just as you would on your regular PC or hardware wallet. There is a big distinction to be made though. The exchange will hold the private keys to this wallet for you. They will undoubtedly do their best to keep your private key secure. But simply put, they are holding your crypto for you. The exchange can potentially be hacked, making your funds vulnerable. They are now custodians of your digital assets and will be acting no differently to your high street bank. Remember the meme I mentioned earlier, 'not your keys not your bitcoin'. Two online exchanges that I am happy to recommend in this book are Kraken and Binance. Kraken is a good place to buy bitcoin with fiat currency and Binance is the place to buy all the other cryptocurrencies with your newly acquired bitcoin. Both these exchanges are very secure and well trusted within the community.

There have been many high-profile hacks of exchanges over the years. This highlights that holding large quantities of cryptocurrencies on exchanges is not good practice. It is acceptable to hold small amounts there or coins that you wish to trade very soon. But for long term storage users should get a PC or hardware wallet (where we ourselves control the private keys and the associated bitcoin). One piece of advice I have heard is that if you are storing more than a few hundred pounds worth of crypto, you should strongly consider using a hardware wallet to secure it. If the user is confident with computers and computer security, they may feel they can manage their private keys themselves on their PC. However, for beginners, non-computer-savvy individuals and especially for people who are holding a large fiat value in crypto I believe a hardware wallet is the way to go. Depending on the make and model a hardware wallet only costs £50-120 and they really do remove much of the stress involved in keeping your cryptocurrency safe. Although you will still have to secure your seed phrase on paper or the Cryptosteel Capsule! On my website https://www.thebitcoinbook.co.uk you will find all of my links for exchanges and products that I recommend in this book, including this one https://www.ledger.com?r=e965d9125b6e a link to buy the Ledger Nano X. This hardware wallet can protect up to 100 different cryptocurrencies at the same time, and not just bitcoin. Ledger, the French company that makes the Nano X, recently received the seal of approval from the National Cyber Security Agency of France (ANSSI).

HOW ARE BITCOIN MADE?

Just like gold, bitcoin are mined, however, Bitcoin miners do not use picks and shovels, they use computing power. Bitcoin miners use specialist machines (also known as Bitcoin miners or mining rigs) to process the transactions on the network. As a thank you for using their machine and electricity, the network rewards them with newly created bitcoin. It is important to note that these are not free bitcoin, as the miners will have used lots of electricity in the process. We will touch on what the mining machines are doing shortly, but for the moment we can just say that they help to manage the network and through their machines work, new bitcoin are issued into circulation.

This process of using electricity and processing power to secure the network and in turn, the minting of new coins, is called proof-of-work (PoW) and is an important and integral part of Bitcoin and many other cryptocurrencies. Another point to note is that these mining machines are quite expensive and can become obsolete after only a couple of years use. This can be through general wear and also by newer, faster models being developed. From as early as 2014, most people believe buying bitcoin directly from an online exchange is easier and possibly cheaper than attempting to mine them. Some companies are now offering a service called cloud mining. This is where the company themselves buy, operate and maintain the mining machine and rent a percentage of the machine's mining power to the paying public. People can sign up for a set period, with the hope to receive a pre-set amount of bitcoin. Buying a cloud mining contract is also deemed unwise by many people. Simply buying the cryptocurrency yourself is seen as a more cost-effective way of spending your currency. Before entering the mining ecosystem, or any part of the cryptocurrency world, the individual needs to undertake as much research as possible.

Don't be dazzled by the bright lights and advertisements claiming 1,234% gains. This includes the wonderful returns claimed by various cloud mining contracts. Do your homework before you part with your government-issued fiat currency. The term used for the issuance of newly created bitcoin is called the block reward. Miners are competing to win the 6.25 newly created bitcoin that are released every ten minutes, this is their incentive to mine. As we just learnt this method of using a machines processing power to help secure the network whilst creating new coins is called proof of work (PoW).

Many cryptocurrencies employ this method; however, many other cryptos use a different system called proof of stake (PoS) which we shall discuss shortly. Some people site PoW systems as wasteful, while others will argue that this level of power usage is needed, especially when it is being used to secure something as powerful and important as the Bitcoin blockchain and the hundreds of billions of pounds currently tied up in it. The function of proof of work mining is another factor that gives Bitcoin (in many people's minds) its value. Earlier we spoke of some of the reasons why Bitcoin has value, well another reason is because of the energy that has been collectively used by the miners to create the 6.25 new coins that are issued every ten minutes. A phenomenal amount of electricity and computational power was used to process all of the transactions in the last block, so it is fair to suggest that these new coins should cost a lot, as lots of power was used to create them. As you can now see the dynamics of how Bitcoin operates is extremely complex, and if you are interested in learning more (or if you are far from sold on the concept) you could search the internet for a better understanding from professionals in the space. Search Google/YouTube for professor Saifedean Ammous or Andreas M. Antonopoulos and include the words PoW or 'where does bitcoin's value come from' and this will point you in the right direction.

Mining rigs are powerful machines, which are designed to do one thing, process numbers extremely fast! The machines are doing something called hashing (see Appendix A) which for all intents and purposes for the layman is processing numbers. Satoshi designed the system to work as follows. Mining machines are racing to find a single and large, random number. Simply put that, is it! All the world's Bitcoin mining machines are hashing trillions upon trillions of numbers per second in the hope they generate a match to this long random number! Once this number has been found, the lucky miner then has the job of attaching the current block of pending transactions to the already existing blockchain. The whole function of Bitcoin mining/transaction validation is far more complicated than I have detailed, however, most of this is automated. From the outside looking in, the mining machines are doing nothing more than playing a fast-paced lottery trying to find that 'lucky' random number. Once the number has been found and the miner has attached the block to the blockchain, they are awarded the newly created 6.25 bitcoin (block reward) and all the associated transaction fees within that block. At this point, the race for a brand new randomly generated number begins all over again, with the miners competing for the next block reward. Miners can mine on their own, which is known as solo mining, or they can group together and form what is known as a mining pool.[13]

There is also something known as the difficulty adjustment. This is yet another clever feature of Bitcoin that makes the finding of this random number, harder or easier, depending on

---

[13] Here miners can pull their resources together and increase the chances of their group 'solving the block'. When an individual's machine within a mining pool solves the block, the bounty is divided up between everyone within the pool, depending on the mining power (aka hashing power) they were contributing. This again is all done automatically, all you need to do is agree to the pool's terms and pay a small fee to the pool operator.

the combined power of all the miners' machines connected to the Bitcoin network at any given time. For various reasons, miners will come and go. Whether that's through machine downtime, power cuts or through general growth of the mining ecosystem as more people try their luck at bitcoin prospecting. Every 2,016 blocks (which is approximately every two weeks) the network automatically adjusts the mining difficulty, so that when the race for each new block reward starts, it is found in roughly ten minutes every time. This function is extremely important and is another reason why Bitcoin is so impressive. This function helps to regulate the minting of new bitcoin. This difficulty regulates the rate at which new blocks will be created, and in turn, the rate at which new bitcoin will be issued into circulation. No matter how much money, equipment and electricity humans push towards creating new bitcoin, the difficulty adjustment will keep the supply rate running true and steady.

The amount of computational power used globally by Bitcoin miners is staggering. It is more accurately referred to as the Bitcoin hash rate and it is soon expected to reach 100 Quintillion hashes per second. This may not sound like a great deal but trust me it is a phenomenal amount of processing power. According to the website 99bitcoins the Bitcoin network is more powerful than the world's 500 biggest supercomputers combined![14] This power is what gives the Bitcoin blockchain its immutability, its strength and its irreversibility, as to attack the Bitcoin blockchain, a person or organisation would need a high percentage of this combined computing power.

---

[14] To put this power into perspective we can look at one of the world's fastest supercomputers, Sequoia. It can process around 16 Petaflops per second, which is 16 quadrillion floating point operations per second (FLOPS). Although massive, this only equates to 1.5% of Bitcoin's total hashing power.

This is a task that even the world's most powerful governments would struggle to muster. Currently, nobody has performed what is known as a 51% attack on Bitcoin.

The process of mining is massively automated, with miners simply attaching their machines to the network and focusing on keeping their machines up and running. Many large companies now operate mining farms as they are referred to. Large warehouses filled with racks and racks of mining machines all connected to the Bitcoin network. These farms and even individuals using one machine, will go to great lengths to keep their machines up and running and cool, as they output masses of heat in the process. As a result of the power used and the heat output, many farms are in regions of the world that have cheap or renewable electricity, and even in colder climates where the cost of cooling the farm is massively reduced.

Monitoring the Bitcoin blockchain, we know at any given moment how many bitcoin there are in circulation and with some clever calculations, we can be (fairly) sure that the last fraction will be mined in the year 2140. Another important factor in Bitcoin mining is that the block reward halves every 210,000 blocks, approximately every four years.

- Originally in 2009, the Bitcoin block reward was 50 bitcoin every block.

- This reduced to 25 after four years.

- The block reward then reduced to 12.5 bitcoin in 2016.

- In May 2020, the block reward dropped to 6.25 bitcoin.

- Four years later it will drop to 3.125 every block.

- Then after another 210,000 blocks in 2028, it will reduce to 1.56250000.

This reduction will continue until the block reward figure whittles down to zero. Remember a bitcoin has eight decimal places, which is why this steady reduction will take some time, over one hundred years in fact. In the far future, once the *last* fraction of the very *last* bitcoin has been mined, it is hoped that Bitcoin miners will happily continue to mine for just the transaction fees alone.[15]

Newcomers to the crypto world are either mortified by the Bitcoin PoW mining process or chomping at the bit to get started themselves. Back in the early days when there were not many people mining bitcoin, it was extremely lucrative as people could mine with a PC using the machine's CPU (Central Processing Unit). After some time, people worked out that the GPU (Graphics Processing Unit) was faster at crunching the numbers, so everyone turned to mining with their graphics cards. This then sparked a wave of people making mining rigs themselves, which were basic computers running multiple graphics cards. After a few short years, big business entered the mining space and companies started to develop specialist chips called ASICs (action specific integrated circuits). Unlike a regular computer chip that is designed to perform various computational tasks, an ASIC is developed to do one thing and to do that one thing very well. So naturally, these early Bitcoin mining pioneers made these ASICs extremely proficient at generating random numbers extremely fast. There then came a three-year-long arms race for better, or faster and faster ASICs. Each time a better chip was developed it gave the lucky miners able to afford the new units an edge when it came to mining with it. This was until enough of the new machines hit the market and the mining difficulty adjusted accordingly.

---

[15] This is on the assumption that the price of an individual coin will have risen significantly, meaning that the comparatively low transaction fees would still be valuable to a miner especially when grouped together with all the other transaction fees within a block.

Existing chip manufacturing techniques have been pushed to their limits thanks to Bitcoin and the ASIC mining revolution. Today, the rate of their advancements has plateaued, and the early days of their importance has normalised just a little, however, they are still the only way to seriously mine Bitcoin. Some other cryptocurrencies only allow their mining to be done using CPU/GPU, believing that approach is fairer and gives the average person a chance to mine. With other popular cryptos having made their coin 'ASIC resistant', meaning even if someone wanted to develop a specific ASIC for that crypto it simply wouldn't work. It is believed that Satoshi wanted a future where all the people of the world could mine, just using their home computers CPU. He simply didn't foresee the profit motives that others would eventually see. Or that people would develop ASICs for Bitcoin mining and that mining itself would evolve into the giant industry it has become. Nowadays if anyone wishes to mine bitcoin, they will need to buy an ASIC mining rig which cost around £1,000-3,000 depending on the model. Using a computer, or GPU rig will be a complete waste of time as your machine will simply not be able to work as fast as the competition, massively reducing your chances of finding that lucky number. All you will do is drive your electricity bill right up, and over time burn out your device in the process through overuse.

One approach that some people employ, is to GPU mine some of the smaller GPU friendly coins and then trade those coins for bitcoin on an exchange. Programs now exist that will do the hard work for you (however you will still need a GPU mining rig). The program can work out which coins are most profitable to mine, through seeing what the cost per coin is and what their networks difficulty is set to. The program will direct your mining rig to work and will constantly switch between the various coins it mines according to these dynamics. Then at the end of the day, with a click of a button, it can sell the multitude of different coins it has mined for you for your chosen favourite, be that bitcoin or whatever the case may be.

At the end of this book, I will include the web address of a company that offers mining rigs that will do just that. Remember though, that with some computer skill you will be able to knock up your own mining rig and with freely available open-source software and forums to learn how, the ability to make your own machine do what was described above will be achievable. There is no such thing as a free lunch, do your homework on mining before you buy a cloud mining contract, machine or attempt to make your own rig!

Before we move on, we will look at the other way that some cryptocurrencies issue new coins and validate their networks transactions. This method does not use the large amounts of electricity and computational power that Bitcoin and many other cryptos utilise. This other approach to securing a network is called proof-of-stake mining (PoS). If you own a PoS cryptocurrency you can do what is called staking. You can set aside all or a portion of your cryptocurrency within your wallet. By effectively locking up your crypto (making it unspendable for the short term) you then become eligible to be a validator for that network. The software behind the cryptocurrency will then determine who gets to validate the transactions on behalf of the network, for the current block being processed. All of this is done automatically. If you are selected, your machine will carry out the task automatically and then after a set period of time (to make sure you haven't cheated in any way), you will regain access to the initial funds that you staked along with your block reward.

Everyone using a cryptocurrency, whether it is a PoW or PoS network will want to trust that it is being managed correctly and is not being abused in any way (that there is consensus or agreement within the network).

The way that both approaches do this is by making people who mine or stake, forfeit something in the process. In PoW cryptocurrencies, miners must forfeit energy (and the initial expense of their mining machine) to take part in the mining process. Yes, there is a reward, but there is also a cost. To be malicious to the Bitcoin network would be expensive and futile, as to hack or to cheat Bitcoin you need lots of money for the electricity and a near-impossible amount of computing power. PoS networks incentivise miners to behave and play by the rules by making them stake their own coins. If a person staking in a PoS network was to interfere with the consensus of their blockchain they would lose their coins.

As PoS cryptocurrencies do not have to solve complex mathematical problems as Bitcoin does, they generally operate faster than Bitcoin and tend to have lower fees. The cost of these benefits is that PoS cryptocurrencies are believed to be less attack proof or resilient than Bitcoin and other PoW coins. The debate over which system is 'better' will continue for some time to come. Maybe these two different types of approaches should not be considered competitors but instead simply different ways of managing different types of networks. If Bitcoin is developing to become a global sized, robust network that can be used as a currency and to store value, many people believe its energy-intensiveness and comparatively slow means of self-management is not a bad thing.

CONSENSUS

One big challenge for all cryptocurrencies is their goal to have consensus (agreement), that the network is up-to-date and all the transactions are valid. The decades' long computer network problem that Satoshi has (probabilistically) solved, is called the Byzantine fault. It takes its name from an ancient allegory, The Byzantines General's Problem. Here we can picture two Byzantine generals preparing to attack a rebel city. Each general has a battalion of soldiers and each is camped on either side of the city. They both need to coordinate so that they attack at the same time, for if they do not their assault will fail, and they will lose the city. How do the generals make sure they both attack at the same time, when they cannot use smoke, fire or flags to signal to one another? They must send messengers on horseback to communicate and relay the order of when to precisely start their advance, along with the acknowledgement of the order. So, if one general sends a message to the other, how does he know his order has arrived safely and has not been intercepted by the enemy and possibly altered? How does the general receiving the order know it is a legitimate order and is from his fellow general and it has not been intercepted by a spy? How does the original general know that the reply he receives is valid and has not been doctored?

In the Bitcoin version of this ancient problem, we replace the battalion of soldiers and generals, with the nodes and miners, and the general's orders become the transaction data. Remember the node operators transmit our transactions to the miners, who themselves are processing the blocks and creating the blockchain. This computer network problem has been unsolved for many decades and is why there is always an element of trust needed in many systems, or for the need for an authority or middleman to manage or control the sensitive 'untrustworthiness' within a network, such as our current banking system. Satoshi designed Bitcoin in such a way, that it cleverly removed the need for any authority. In the crypto space, this has spawned a new meaning for the word, trustless. Yes, we as users *can* trust it, we can trust that it is safe to use and store our bitcoin, but I don't have to trust the miners and node operators, or other users for that matter. As all the participants within the Bitcoin network are simply 'forced' into using Bitcoin in a safe, trusted, and moral way by the software and architecture of the system. Satoshi hasn't completely solved the Byzantine fault but came *very* close and designed Bitcoin in such a way that it is *extremely* unlikely that the network can be gamed or cheated, and the information within the blockchain altered. For as we shall learn in a moment when the miners add a new block to the blockchain, it becomes harder still for the information before it to be altered. Every ten minutes when a new block is added to the ever-growing blockchain, it makes it infinitely harder to alter information further down the chain. This way of managing consensus, without the need for an authority or trusted third party is another one of the many reasons why Bitcoin is so special.

CONFIRMATIONS

When you send bitcoin to an address, it is generally received within a few seconds to a minute or so. However, it is good practice to wait a while, to make sure that it has definitely arrived and has been properly processed. (A bit like how it takes a few days for a traditional cheque to clear, it also takes a little time for a bitcoin transaction to clear). This time delay is referred to as confirmations. When a bitcoin transaction is initially sent, it firstly sits in a group, or pool of unconfirmed transactions, known as a mempool. Here it sits, waiting for miners to scoop it up and add it into the block that they are processing. During this time while it sits unconfirmed (before being officially added to the blockchain), it is possible that a scammer can quickly try to spend that same bitcoin again. They can attempt what is called a double-spend attack.

The double-spend attack has been a long-running issue that has stopped many digital currencies from ever leaving the drawing board. Satoshi designed a clever mechanism for protecting against this and it is called confirmations. The bitcoin will likely arrive in your wallet very quickly, but it will not become part of your spendable balance until a set amount of confirmations have passed. When a new block is added to the blockchain, it serves as a confirmation to all the transactions in the blocks before it. The more confirmations you have, (meaning the more blocks that are on top of 'your' block) the more credible your transaction has become, and it makes the chances of a double-spend attack infinitely less likely. This confirmation time is neatly handled by your wallet software. If you are receiving bitcoin from someone you know and trust, you can rest assured that you have the bitcoin as soon as it has landed into your wallet, however, the wallet software obviously cannot distinguish between people you do and do not know, and will still wait until a few confirmations have passed before this transaction becomes part of your spendable balance.

General agreement within the space regarding Bitcoin payments is that individuals and merchants should allow for at least 6 confirmations to completely trust that the payment is (virtually) 100% valid. This may seem a lot, to wait for 6 x 10 minute-blocks, but experience has taught people to stick to this figure, as some users have been caught out trusting fewer confirmations. You may find that many people are happy to wait for 0-3 confirmations, while others will want to wait for 4-6 or even more. The number of confirmations a person will want to wait for will depend on several factors; these will include things like:

- How well you know the individual or organisation paying you.

- How trustworthy they are.

- The price of the item being purchased.

- How serious/upsetting it would be if their payment was not legitimate and the person you were trading with 'drove off with your goods'.

As an example of this, should you use bitcoin to buy a £10 T-shirt from an online store, the merchant may happily start to process your order instantly. By the time 2-3 confirmations have passed, they may well be ready to post your item and be happy to do so. However, if you are using bitcoin to buy an expensive item such as a holiday, the salesperson will most likely want at least 6 confirmations before handing you the tickets, to satisfy themselves that the transaction is near to 100% valid and that there is a near-zero chance they're going to end up with egg on their face. If you're lucky enough to be buying an extremely expensive item, such as a Lamborghini or an around the world cruise, it is conceivable that the representative will require a couple more confirmations than the standard 6. I have even heard in some rare cases, that organisations who deal with unbelievably high amounts may wish to wait for 100 confirmations. Your average individual need not worry too much about confirmations, as our wallet software will not let you spend newly received bitcoin until enough confirmations have passed and it is cleared into your spendable balance. Once it is part of your spendable balance in your crypto wallet, it is yours to keep or to spend. This confirmation time may seem annoying, but it does potentially save people being cheated. I admit that on face value this time delay does seem to be a limitation, especially as other cryptos can operate faster, although many people believe this time delay is a feature and not a bug. Sound/hard money needs to be robust and this 'slowness' is one facet that makes Bitcoin special and secure. It needs to be secure if it is going to have any chance of competing as a modern, digital global currency or store of value and grow to be worth trillions of pounds. Having said all of this I believe many merchants will happily trade with low confirmations, especially if the item is fairly cheap in the first place and even more so if they know the customer.

The crypto space is forever moving at breakneck speed and a new development called The Lightning Network or just Lightning for short, has made instant/no confirmation payments a reality. This separate software that works in conjunction with Bitcoin, allows people to happily send bitcoin in an untrusted manner, extremely fast and with zero confirmations. Lightning is active now but not many people are using it just yet. Before too long, it could become widespread and Bitcoin will become even more amazing than it already is. The Lightning Network will also allow for micropayments and nanopayments to become a reality. Micropayments are payments that are less than a penny, while nanopayments can be as small as a thousandth of a penny! Using these types of payments, people will be able to instantly pay for music or video streams by the second or to read articles or whatever the case may be. It could open great possibilities for individuals and companies to monetise their content and services. Tipping small amounts will now become possible again using this new technology. Incidentally, you remember the story of Laszlo and his pizza purchase from earlier. Well, it is reported that he also purchased the world's first pizza using the Bitcoin Lightning Network. The micro/nanopayment opportunities that Bitcoin and other cryptocurrencies can offer are fascinating and at the same time very futuristic. Some of you may already be familiar with the term Internet of Things (IoT). This is where our electronic devices are becoming smarter and having internet connectivity added as standard. Shortly all our devices will be communicating to us directly or to each other. In a simple and already publicised example, smart refrigerators can remind their owners when certain sundries are in short supply, with the option for the fridge to order the required shopping itself. It is not just humans paying for streaming services, or fridges buying your milk where micro/nanopayments will be useful, but also for the coming machine economy. From our future smart cars paying for toll lane access, through to actual machine to machine payments. A future where drones and robots can pay for their own maintenance or even hire themselves out to humans or other machines is an eye-opening prospect. Other cryptocurrencies now available are already lining themselves up for this very function, with a few of the popular ones being IOTA, VeChain and WaltonChain. Thanks to developments such as The Lightning Network, bitcoin payments are also now suitable for this future robotic economy.

Saifedean Ammous raises another good point in his book *The Bitcoin Standard,* which relates to confirmation time. Yes, we may have to wait for 6 blocks to be sure the bitcoin is truly ours, but compared to the legacy banking system, this is quite fast. We believe that because our government currency appears to move in seconds at the chip and pin device that it is fast.

The fact that in shops, bars and restaurants we can now swipe and walk on compounds the illusion that our currency is fast and even efficient, however huge risks are taken on by the banks and credit card companies involved and fraud is rampant. The bankers know that in most cases their bank to bank settlements will be honoured, but unknown to most people and depending on the type of transaction, true final settlement can take anywhere between 3-30 days to complete by the institutions involved in our legacy transactions. We are swiping digits to one another, almost willy-nilly believing our system is fast, however, it takes the banks days or even weeks to eventually settle, with some of these organisations settling in gold if necessary. Saifedean shows us that Bitcoin has allowed for the first time, final settlement of a bearer asset to be completed in just *one* hour. A system that even the banks, governments and central banks of the world can use and trust, even if they do not trust one another.

THE LIGHTNING NETWORK

As just mentioned, the Lightning Network (LN) is a new technology, which is hoping to help Bitcoin scale to become a fast and secure global payment solution. The idea was first conceived in 2015 by Joseph Poon and Thaddeus Dryja. It is a separate technology to Bitcoin; however, it is used in conjunction with the Bitcoin network to help speed up transactions and reduce fees.

Using the internet as a quick example, we can see how *it* has different systems or protocols, that are stacked on top of each other. We think of the internet as solely being websites, which is the protocol HTTP (HyperText Transfer Protocol). Well, the internet is more than just HTTP. Email (SMTP) and file transfer (FTP) are also a part of the internet and are stacked on top of the internet's base protocol. Various other protocols sit on top of each other to allow the internet as we know it today, to function as it does.

Bitcoin will evolve similarly with different technologies or layers, stacking up on top of each other to increase the functionality of the system. The Bitcoin blockchain is sometimes referred to as the base chain or base protocol and even sometimes as layer 1. Lightning is referred to as a layer 2 technology. I will not focus massively on Lightning in this chapter as readers who wish to enter the Bitcoin economy will do so at the base level. They will likely visit an exchange mentioned in this book and buy bitcoin and store these coins either in their own wallet or with the exchange.

In the coming months and years, however, as Bitcoin adoption increases, the public, by and large, will start to utilise Lightning more and more to help facilitate their transfers. People will still be able to send their bitcoin to one another directly on the base chain, the Bitcoin blockchain, however, it will become a lot cheaper and faster to use layer 2 solutions such as Lightning. In the coming years (if Lightning adoption continues) it will become second nature to use Lightning or other layer 2 or even layer 3 solutions. Many existing Bitcoin wallets are already offering Lightning payment options. To briefly detail how Lightning works, users open what is called a channel with another Lightning user, be that a friend or family member or institution. In doing so they make an initial bitcoin transaction on the Bitcoin blockchain. This effectively locks that bitcoin into the channel and then allows you to send that bitcoin using Lightning.

On LN the denomination of Satoshi's or sats has been fully adopted. So, once you have bitcoin locked into your Lightning channel, you can send sats to other people on the network in a near-instant manner, with no need for confirmations (because the initial transaction/required confirmations have already happened on the blockchain). Sats are transmitted to the end recipient, sometimes directly (if you have a direct channel open with them), or if you don't, the sats are routed instantly through the interconnecting web of pre-existing channels on the Lightning Network. This is all done instantaneously and with zero trust needed by any of the participants.

Let's leave our Lightning lesson there for today as like I said, most readers of this book will not be using LN for the foreseeable future. Not until they have already well and truly established themselves in the ecosystem and are fully comfortable with basic bitcoin transactions. Just remember though that technologies like Lightning will allow for higher transactions per second and also lower fees.

The podcast series called *What Bitcoin Did* has a beginner's series on Bitcoin that I would recommend to those readers who would like to learn additional information and from other people's perspectives.[16]

---

[16] Each episode covers a different aspect of Bitcoin with each featuring a different professional. Episode #13 is with the bright young developer, Jack Mallards and is all about LN. He tries to explain the technology simply but at times it does get a little technical and even a little rude. I would recommend listening to this beginner's series from the start and in order.

WHAT IS A FORK?

Bitcoin was the first of its kind. There are now thousands of other cryptocurrencies, digital assets and cryptographic tokens that have followed in its wake. Many of these are copies of Bitcoin, while some are copies of the other leading cryptocurrencies. We will not focus too much on forks, as it is something that the developers, node operators and miners deal with, so for this reason, I shall generalise a little to keep things simple. Forks occur when someone changes the Bitcoin software, when a rule or parameter is adjusted and as a result, a new version of the software is created. There are primarily two types of forks, soft and hard. A soft fork is comparable to a software update whereas a hard fork is a little more serious and ordinarily results in a brand new coin and a new blockchain sprouting into existence. Just as a fork in a path splits into two new paths, a cryptocurrency hard fork can be visualised similarly with a *new* blockchain forking off in a separate direction at the moment the fork takes place (while the original blockchain continues in its direction). In 2017 there was a highly controversial fork of Bitcoin. This created a new coin and blockchain that was confusingly named Bitcoin Cash. Not to be mistaken with *Bitcoin* the cryptocurrency we are primarily focusing on within this book. We will look a little closer at this new crypto in the coming pages as you need to understand the history and difference between it and Bitcoin, as it is believed that many unfortunate newcomers have mistakenly bought Bitcoin Cash believing it was Bitcoin and I don't want you to make the same mistake.

Congratulations are in order! Especially if you have made it this far through this book without wanting to throw it into the bin. I hope you have enjoyed your journey down the cryptocurrency rabbit hole. You should especially congratulate yourself if, like me, you are not particularly technically minded and have kept up with what you have read. You should be quite proud of yourself as you now know more about Bitcoin than 99% of the world's population! You are now duly awarded your Bitcoin Blue Belt. This belt is meant to signify the blue sky, which the plant continues to grow toward becoming stronger and beginning to possess a more confident presence. Now that you have some more appreciation of the technology behind Bitcoin, you may be interested to learn the story of the limestone discs called Rai stones that I mentioned at the start of this book.[17] Now we are ready to continue to part three of this book and the last few chapters, the ones that will help those of you interested in getting your hands on some bitcoin! We will learn about exchanges and some basic security measures needed to protect these digital assets. We will also talk about some of the other top coins out there, so you have a better understanding of what's on offer in this new economy. So, let's re-enter the crypto dojo and start preparing for your Bitcoin Black Belt.

---

[17] This link will take you to a short article on how Bitcoin has borrowed techniques from a thousand-year-old, stone money, which the islanders from Yap used.
www.sciencealert.com/the-original-bitcoin-still-exists-as-giant-stone-money-on-a-tiny-pacific-island

PART III

THE NEW ECONOMY AWAITS YOU

ALTERNATIVE COINS

As we learnt in the first part of this book, Bitcoin is based on digital software and it is open source, meaning everyone can see the inner workings and freely use its code. With some knowledge and time, you can copy the Bitcoin software and create a new cryptocurrency. Or with some extra skill, you can write your own software, and create your own unique crypto. To date, there are now over 3,000 other cryptocurrencies available on the market. Not all of them are direct copies of Bitcoin, but many share similarities. When creating a new coin, the developers get to choose all its features, such as the total amount that will be created, along with the speed of their release, how it will be mined along with many more functions. In this chapter, we will take a little look at three coins that are vastly different from bitcoin.

As we are starting to learn more about some of the other cryptocurrencies out there, now might be a good time to mention that the names of these individual cryptocurrencies can be shortened down to a few letters, just the same way that stocks and shares have their ticker symbols. For example, AAPL is Apple's stock ticker symbol, TSLA is Tesla's and AMZN is Amazon's. Cryptocurrency has adopted the same system.

On the cryptocurrency exchanges, forums or in general internet chatter, you may see these used interchangeably with their names. Someone may refer to Bitcoin as Bitcoin or its ticker symbol which is BTC.

All the cryptocurrencies that came after Bitcoin are referred to as altcoins, this stands for alternative coins. Many altcoins behave similarly to Bitcoin, while others are vastly different. Some are competing with Bitcoin to become a currency or store of value, while others are offering new and exciting ways of revamping and shaking up many sectors, from the legal sector, gaming, supply chain management, gambling, insurance, identity, storing house deeds, managing music artists rights, storing medical records and much more.

Ether (ETH)

Our first altcoin is from an organisation called Ethereum. Their coin is called ether and is very different from bitcoin. It isn't planning to become a currency per se, but a unit that powers a new type of applications platform. These apps are called DApps (pronounced Dee-apps) which stands for decentralised applications. They are similar to the regular apps that we currently use on our devices, however, they are decentralised meaning that they are not stored on centralised systems/servers such as Google Play or the Apple Store where they can be censored and easily deleted. They are stored on a decentralised network and shared P2P (peer to peer) and because of this, they are censorship-resistant. Another area that Ethereum is feverishly working on is a technology called smart contracts. A smart contract is not written by a lawyer and signed with an expensive fountain pen but is written by a developer using computer code. It then uses the Ethereum blockchain to manage, execute and settle these contracts. This might sound boring on the face of it, however, the possibilities of these contracts are quite fascinating, should they become widely adopted.

As a trendy example and possible future use case of a smart contract, we can imagine a rock band having just recorded their latest album. Using this technology, they could sit down and between themselves decide how they wish the royalties to be divided between the various members of the group each time the songs were played on the radio/TV. The smart contract can be carefully crafted, so much so, that the individual band members would receive their cut of ether automatically every time the song was aired across the world. The contract could even instantly perform the transaction! If say the drummer wrote a particular song within the album, (and the band all agreed that when that particular song was played his/her cut would be X% larger than normal) the smart contract could be designed to act on this and would pay them accordingly.

If perfected, this new technology could be used throughout many industries, but will massively disrupt the legal sector, just like Bitcoin is disrupting the financial sector. Like bitcoin, ether's price has also climbed massively over the last few years. Many other cryptocurrencies are competing in the DApp/smart contract space, including Cardano, Tron, Neo, and EOS.

Vechain (VET)

This coin is tackling the supply chain management sector. They have spent lots of time partnering with many big names including PricewaterhouseCoopers, BMW, the National Research Consulting Centre of China, China Unicom, Kuehne & Nagel, People's Insurance Company of China and many more multi-billion pound organisations. They offer a few different services, but their main focus is on supply chain management solutions. It was created by Sunny Lu, a former Louis Vuitton division chief who was witness to the damage fake products can cause brands. It is reported that in China 30,000 bottles of fake imported wine are opened every hour, and that your average bottle of champagne has been refilled and sealed with fake champagne up to seven times. VeChains solution for the drinks industry was to develop a seal that stops wine counterfeiters in their tracks.

Another supply chain solution pushed them to develop small electronic chips that can be added to a product at the point of manufacture, which is then tracked throughout the entire supply chain, to the end customer. This enables all parties to check the VeChain blockchain to confirm the validity of the product and ensure its integrity. Their services and technology are being used by the Chinese government in Shanghai, to track and authenticate their vaccines as well as preventing the spread of counterfeits, along with monitoring electric vehicle use. Another big use for the small chips is brand protection applications worldwide within the fashion industry.

MaidSafeCoin (MAID)

MaidSafe is the name of the Scottish company behind this project. It has been actively developed by David Irvine and his team for over ten years. MaidSafe stands for: *Massive Array of Internet Disks – Secure Access for Everyone.*

Their goal is an audacious one, as they intend to make a new decentralised and autonomous network, which translates into a safer and more privacy driven internet. Not only that, but it will include file storage, email capabilities along with many other services. In their words 'no more hacked data, no more stolen passwords and eavesdropping. Private. Secure. Anonymous'. The invention of cryptocurrency has allowed them to perfect their product, which in turn sent them back to the drawing board for a complete redesign. Development is still ongoing but with much of the network complete, testing is now underway, and a user-ready product is believed to be with us soon. Their coin MaidSafeCoin will be used for interacting with the services that the platform provides.

As with all the various cryptocurrency projects out there, whether it is a currency, smart contract platform, a blockchain that manages supply chains or decentralised file storage, remember there are multiple teams all working on similar products, racing to be the first to market and striving to gain the largest customer base. A final point to note in this chapter is that the word altcoin is seen as a derogatory term for some people. They find it insulting that any coin developed after Bitcoin is labelled with this term, as it generally belittles the coin in question, implying it is a worthless copy or imitation of Bitcoin. Some people view a high percentage of the 3,000 plus coins now available as being *worthless* and having little to no purpose. Indeed, a development team can quickly design a coin and cash in on the new crypto/blockchain craze and make a quick buck. However, in the eyes of others, many of these altcoins are legitimate and do seem to have a worthy use case. Therefore, the community that favour a particular coin does not like the altcoin term. Soon we shall take a broader look at some of the top cryptocurrencies out there so that newcomers have a glimpse of what is available in the wider crypto market. However, it is important to remember, that just as Bitcoin's future is unclear the very same must be said for the multitude of other coins out there. Many of these different uses for blockchain tech could fizzle out or not become workable for a whole range of different reasons. Bitcoin has a couple of things going for it with regards to its future. One is that it has the first movers' advantage and has a good head start on many of the newer coins. It is decentralised, whereas many of the newer generations are not. It also has the most adoption, largest market cap and most hashing power. But all these facts could change, nothing is certain and newcomers to this economy would be wise to take their time when entering the sweet shop that is this new cryptocurrency marketplace.

WHAT IS BITCOIN CASH (BCH)?

In August 2017 Bitcoin was forked and a new coin was created called Bitcoin Cash (BCH). It should not be confused with the original Bitcoin (BTC), as they both have their own separate blockchains and are totally different! So why was Bitcoin Cash created, or B-Cash as it is referred to by some people who didn't agree with the fork?

Bitcoin has suffered a scaling issue over the last couple of years. Meaning that it has struggled, if that is the right term, to keep up with the adoption that it has experienced. This is not uncommon with new technologies and if anything, it shows that Bitcoin is offering something that people do want.

Bitcoin is not the only cryptocurrency that has suffered from scaling issues. The reason for the fork all came down to the size of each block within the blockchain. Satoshi set the block size to 1 Megabyte (Mb) and knew it would most likely have to increase as the network grew, or an additional scaling solution would be needed, as you can only fit a certain amount of transactions into a 1Mb block. In 2017, a Bitcoin improvement increased the block size to a maximum of 2Mb (with a theoretical limit of 4Mb). We should note that block size issue is a problem for all cryptocurrencies (that utilise a blockchain). One reason is that if the blocks are too big, over time the entire blockchain becomes too large and costly for the node operators and miners to store. Other concerns are that larger blocks could lead to mining centralisation, as well as lowering the security of the network. Some experts will disagree with these three points, which is exactly why the 'block size war' raged for so long.

If there are too many transactions trying to fit into the current block being processed, then some transactions will have to wait for the following block. This means a further ten-minute delay, which is not ideal for a payment system that is supposed to be competing on some degree with the current system.

As adoption grew, so did the demand for transaction space within the blocks. Blocks started to become filled, which started to cause transaction delays on the blockchain. Everyone thought the solution was simple, just increase the block size, to allow more transactions in. The lead developers, influencers and businesses then got stuck in what became a two-year-long battle. They were trying to agree on how and when to do it, and most importantly, what size the new blocks should be. Another point to note is that as a result of these delays to the network, the transaction fees started to rise. Bitcoin was originally developed to become a global payments system. One that could (and possibly still will) handle both large and small transactions alike, but as the transaction fees started to climb, it ruled out the possibility of bitcoin being used for small transactions. As a result of blocks becoming full, the miners were incentivised to increase the fees. If you wanted your transaction to be processed straight away, you had to bear the increased transaction fee. If you didn't mind the transaction sitting in limbo for a couple of hours or longer, you could set a far lower fee. All these delays fuelled a chain reaction of increasing fees, further delays, and the ensuing arguments. Long after the block-war finished, people have since analysed the 'transactional bloat' to the Bitcoin blockchain and many people believe that much of this was artificially created and was most likely caused by proponents of the 'larger block solution', by creating multiple small transactions to fill the blocks on purpose. This is not to say that blocks wouldn't have become full at some point, just that the 2017 blockchain bloat the community experienced may not have been organic.

So, what is Bitcoin Cash (BCH)? It is pretty much the same as Bitcoin (BTC), aside from being a different coin and having a different blockchain. It has an increased block size of 32Mb, and it also doesn't currently utilise the Lightning Network. Aside from that, there is little to distinguish the two, it still has a cap of 21 million coins and is still used the same way as Bitcoin.

Its blockchain has recorded the same transactions as Bitcoin (up until the moment the fork took place). After the fork, its blockchain has now recorded its own transactions and it is now completely separate to Bitcoin's blockchain. So why were many people so upset by the fork? It divided the community for one thing. Many felt that it wasn't necessary, as it is believed that the Bitcoin developers would solve the scaling issue in due course. It has confused new people entering the crypto space by having two coins with such similar names. In the days leading up to the fork, there was mass uncertainty on what would happen, as Bitcoin had never had a hard fork forced upon it in such a way before. Even experts in the space were unsure of what would happen. Would one or both coins/blockchains crash and burn? Would the Bitcoin miners leave and migrate their mining machines to the new BCH blockchain? As it turned out both survived and BCH still survives today. However, the arguments still rage, now focusing primarily on which one is the 'real' Bitcoin. In most people's opinion, including my own, the original Bitcoin (BTC) is the real Bitcoin, this seems logical in my opinion. BTC still holds the majority share of the two (as it is worth more and has more mining power). It was also the first coin to market and the first to claim the name Bitcoin. For the BCH followers, it is a matter of technicalities as they believe their coin is more in keeping with the original vision that Satoshi had. Therefore, they believe their new network is the real Bitcoin and BTC should roll over and make way for the new iteration. Only time will tell how the two will develop, coexist and become adopted.

Soon after the fork, BCH adoption slowly started to grow. With many companies adopting BCH as a payment option due to the fact the transaction fees were lower than BTC. Some companies even removed BTC as a payment option altogether, as at the time BTC fees increased massively and it became almost impractical to use for many payments.

Shortly after the fork, fees on the BTC blockchain normalised again. As time marched on, BCH slowly started to lose the price it had originally gained and in my opinion, it also seems to have lost much of its support which was fairly thin to begin with. Many people also believe that a lot of the transactional data we see from BCH is being faked. The theory is a few wealthy individuals are purposefully sending coins back and forth to one another to make it look like the coin and its blockchain is being used a lot, and that these people are even spending millions of dollars a month to keep the price high and ranked in the top ten (to make it look like the coin is being adopted by the public at large).

Bitcoin (BTC) does have a few tricks up its sleeve. It has many more active developers than BCH, along with a continuous push to constantly better itself and make BTC more robust and usable for the world. The developers are still very hesitant to raise the block size any more than they already have. However, many new protocols have been developed to speed up the network while keeping the block size small. One such protocol is called SegWit and it allows less data to be stored in the transaction itself, along with the technology Lightning that we mentioned earlier, which helps to speed up Bitcoin by allowing for zero-confirmation transactions. If only the Bitcoin Cash developers had waited another year or two, maybe the promise of the LN itself would have settled the debate and have made the fork unnecessary. Many people believe that by jumping straight to 32Mb Bitcoin Cash will soon have its own problems to deal with, as all this extra size means that the nodes and miners must store more data, which ultimately costs them more fiat currency.

Another point worth mentioning is that the moment the fork took place, all holders of BTC automatically received an equal amount of BCH. That is how most blockchain forks distribute their coins, by issuing the new coin to people that are holding the original coin. The reason for this is the instant a fork takes place, the new blockchain is momentarily identical to the original chain and all the coins on the original chain are then duplicated onto the newer chain. If you had half a bitcoin at the time of the fork you automatically received 0.5 BCH.

This issuance of 'free' BCH furthered the buzz. People holding lots of BTC became even wealthier within a blink of an eye. Many quickly sold their freely received BCH, as they believed its price would quickly plummet. They assumed that the coin was not going to be adopted. This idea of free crypto from nowhere then went on to spark a craze of other Bitcoin forks.

Other developers quickly saw that they too could create a fork and tried their chances of mimicking what BCH had done. The community at large only just tolerated the BCH fork. In my opinion, most of the other forks are far from credible and are referred to by some people as 'money grabs'. Many are seen as scams, that are simply piggybacking off Bitcoin's success, in the hope to create a new coin that they may quickly sell for profit. After the BCH fork, there was the Bitcoin Gold (BTG) fork. I do not know much about Bitcoin Gold. However, the community by and large seem to tolerate it, at least more than they do BCH. This in part, might be due to the attitude and demeanour of one of the main BCH proponents Roger Ver. Originally a Bitcoin maximalist (see Appendix A) who did lots of good in the space, he even earnt himself the nickname Bitcoin Jesus. He was the most public and vocal spokesperson behind the BCH movement and now vehemently promotes it. His old nickname has been replaced by the Bitcoin community to Bitcoin Judas. He owns the Bitcoin.com domain but confusingly (and to many Bitcoiners, annoyingly) promotes BCH on this site. Some people in the community refer to Bitcoin Cash as B-Cash because they know how much that name annoys Roger. In retaliation, BCH followers call Bitcoin, Bitcoin Core (which strictly speaking is the correct name for the

Bitcoin software that Satoshi developed. Many Bitcoiners themselves also refer to Bitcoin as Bitcoin Core).

It can get a little confusing at the best of times, as sometimes Roger will refer to BTC as Bitcoin Core and BCH as Bitcoin (dropping the word cash) because in his mind BCH *is* Bitcoin. To date, there have been over 50 forks of Bitcoin! To name a few there is Bitcoin Diamond/Oil/Plus/Faith/Pizza/Super and Atom. Some of these could be legitimate but I feel that most are a waste of time and could just be trying to make a quick buck. There are so many coins out there now and only so many hours in the day, making it impossible (for me at least) to fully understand all the coins various use cases, along with their stats and development plans.

Approximately 18 months after Bitcoin Cash was launched, the people involved started to disagree on how the BCH project should develop. This infighting ended in yet another fork. That's right folks, Bitcoin Cash itself was forked and created yet another Bitcoin, or more strictly speaking another Bitcoin Cash! The original Bitcoin Cash (BCH) kept that name while the new coin's ticker symbol is BSV. Standing for Bitcoin Satoshi's Vision, as they believe *their* coin is the true Bitcoin and is what Satoshi would have wanted Bitcoin to become. I don't know much about BSV aside from that the main proponent of this project is Dr Craig Wright. This is the person who since 2016 has claimed that he *is* Satoshi Nakamoto! This is something that the real Satoshi could do quite simply by moving some of his many bitcoin. Wright has not been able to do that and any evidence he has provided has been quickly tested and debunked by the community. He then started legal proceedings against people in the space who have publicly voiced their opinion that he is not Satoshi. His actions have led to a fierce backlash from some big players in the space. Firstly, from the CEO of Binance, one of the largest crypto exchanges, who threatened to delist BSV from their exchange if Wright did not drop the matter and stop his legal actions. He didn't and a week later Binance did indeed drop BSV deposits to their exchange.

In June 2020 an individual proved irrevocably that they own many of the addresses that Craig Wright submitted to a court, claiming to be his. For many people, this has now cemented the fact that Wright is not Satoshi, and that he has been lying for many years.

Roger Ver owns and operates the website Bitcoin.com (so do not visit that site as you may be fooled into buying BCH). Bitcoin.org is a different site, but the control and direction of this site is also being tested, as it is believed the individual in control is also swinging towards BCH. If you would like to learn more about Bitcoin (BTC) via the internet, please visit some of the sites I reference at the end of this book.

I apologise for any confusion, but these stories only highlight how people are scrambling for power and money in this space, and at times seem happy to hurt this new economy for personal gain. Like all the information in this book, it has been a basic overview of the subject. Further education will be needed for those who wish to learn the full story about forks and BCH/BSV. Remember that this book is primarily focused on the original, oldest, grandfather of all cryptocurrencies, the OG and grandmaster that is Bitcoin (BTC).

SOME NEGATIVE OPINIONS

While we are on a bit of a downer from the last chapter, let us continue with the negative vibe for a few more paragraphs. I would not feel comfortable if I didn't briefly mention some of the negative views that some people have of Bitcoin. I would feel rotten if a reader of this book bought some bitcoin or any other cryptocurrency, solely on the merits I have presented and then for whatever reason the crypto market flopped, and they lost their fiat currency. Like any new technology, there are positives and negatives and Bitcoin is no different. That's why there has been such an explosion of other coins in its wake, as people have tried to develop a coin that doesn't have a particular feature of Bitcoin, or improves on an existing one or replaces it with a different one altogether. It is fair to say that I am a big fan of Bitcoin, however, I am not 100% blinkered and do appreciate some of the larger community's concerns, even though I may not fully agree with all of them. I will list just a few of the main concerns that I am aware of and am sure if you do your investigating you will find more.

There are a few people in the space who believe that the 21 million coin limit should be increased. It will upset lots of people if the limit that Satoshi set in place is not respected, as it will reduce the scarcity of the coins and in turn most likely reduce the price (albeit hopefully for the short term). One of the people who is promoting this idea is Peter Todd one of the lead developers of Bitcoin. It is speculated that this could be achieved by slackening the rules around the block reward halving every 4 years. However, it is *extremely* unlikely to ever happen and in my opinion, would most likely result in a new cryptocurrency forking off Bitcoin rather than Bitcoin changing such a fundamental aspect of its protocol.

Too many people have entered the Bitcoin ecosystem on the understanding that only 21 million coins will ever exist. I am confident, as others are, that this figure will be respected. On a side note, because there are so many Satoshi's in a single coin (100 million) it means there are going to be a total of 4 Quadrillion (4 million, trillions) Satoshi's in total, once the last bitcoin is mined. This figure of total units is many times greater than all the world's currencies combined. So simply put, 4 Quadrillion units should happily serve humanity for the foreseeable future.

Bitcoin can only muster a small number of transactions per second. This issue was one of the reasons Bitcoin Cash forked from Bitcoin, as bigger blocks allow for more transactions. Today Bitcoin can handle roughly 7 transactions per second (TPS). Note: This figure may be higher at your time of reading. Many other cryptocurrencies are in a similar position, with a relatively low TPS. Ethereum is also battling to increase its transactional capabilities, which are currently stuck at around 15 TPS. Visa on the other hand, which is managed in a different way to Bitcoin (that being a centralised network, where trust is not needed and fraud occurs every second on their network), can perform around 20,000 TPS. Many of the new generation cryptocurrencies are striving to outperform Bitcoin in this area, with many boasting they can, but then struggling to come up with the goods once their coin is up and running. NEO is one cryptocurrency that has a high TPS of between 1,000-10,000 and believes it will push 100,000 TPS shortly. IOTA is another coin with high throughput, but this cryptocurrency does not utilise a blockchain. As we know Bitcoin now has Lightning, which is slowly being adopted and making faster transactions possible. It is believed by some people that in the future the lightning network could scale massively and allow for as much as 1,000,000 TPS.

Bitcoin's lack of total privacy is seen as a limitation by some people and they wish to add new protocols to help make it more private. While other people who also like Bitcoin, are enjoying the fact that businesses/regulators are happy with its openness and wish to keep it as it is. There could be a point in the future where the developers, miners or users start to disagree on how this should be addressed. This could result in another fork of Bitcoin and the development of a new coin that is like Bitcoin but with more privacy built-in from the start. There are many developments in the Bitcoin space and privacy is slowly being addressed by many of the developers.

Another benefit of Lightning is that it increases privacy for its users. However, as we shall soon see, coins already exist that are more private than Bitcoin and it is feasible that if Bitcoin does not become more private, these coins will fulfil that role if people wish to send anonymous transactions. These coins are labelled privacy coins and to name a few we have Monero, Dash, Zcash and Pivx.

We have learnt that Bitcoin is decentralised, and how it is a team of developers, educators and advanced users who help to progress Bitcoin. However, there are concerns that the mining aspect within Bitcoin is no longer decentralised and over the last few years, a handful of wealthy individuals have cornered the mining market. This is a little sad especially as Satoshi wanted a future where individuals around the world were able and capable to mine bitcoin with their PC. She would be sad to see that it has turned into a big business. China is the most prominent player in Bitcoin mining. This is for two reasons; they have the cheapest electricity and it is also where most of the planets chip manufacturing plants are. The closer the mining farms are to where the mining chips are produced the better the financial returns. In 2019 the Chinese government released details on how they intended to ban Bitcoin mining.

Since then they have reversed this intention and their history of banning then unbanning many aspects of cryptocurrency continues. The latest unbanning was coupled with an extremely positive countrywide push for blockchain technology. It seems that the Chinese government are planning to adopt blockchain, not necessarily Bitcoin but certainly blockchain tech. So, would a large country banning mining affect Bitcoin? The fact that Bitcoin mining itself is regulated by the difficulty adjustment that we mentioned earlier, a move by China (or any other country) to ban mining should have little to no effect on Bitcoin. It would still be as secure, even if an entire country turned off their machines. Many pundits believe that wealthy miners would simply move to mining-friendly shores. Others would just sell their rigs to people in nations who can legally mine. Sanctions like this would only push many people into mining illegally as for some, the profits are too good to pass up on. India has also had a rocky history with Bitcoin, and like China keep banning then unbanning aspects of Bitcoin. With a recent bill planning to severely outlaw Bitcoin and fine people the equivalent of £10,000 for owning and even just promoting it. Recent reports are that the proposal of this bill has been dropped. In the case of China and India, some people will not stop using Bitcoin just because a power-hungry government decide they wish to make it illegal. The prohibition laws in America from 1920-33 along with countless other examples throughout history help to prove that case.

An American Congressman called Brad Sherman has joined the list of US politicians calling for an outright ban of Bitcoin and all cryptocurrencies; however, I am sure his demands will fall on deaf ears and at most, will only result in stronger regulation of cryptocurrencies in his country. It was recently uncovered that one of his largest donation contributors is a large traditional currency processor. America has been slow to regulate countrywide, but their *BitLicence* regulation that requires all New York located Bitcoin companies to apply for the costly licence, only forced the majority of companies to move to other parts of the US, as well as other crypto-friendly countries such as Japan, Hong Kong, Singapore, Malta, The Isle of Man, Bermuda, Dubai and many countries across Europe. The list of countries that have made Bitcoin illegal includes Ecuador, Bolivia, Algeria, Egypt, Morocco, Nepal, and Pakistan. In Vietnam and Indonesia, it is legal to trade and hold bitcoin but illegal to use it as a payment tool. Eleven countries have some sort of banking ban/restriction however it is still legal. Most of the countries in the world do allow their citizens to use Bitcoin.

Some people fear that when quantum computers become reality it will enable people to hack Bitcoin instantly. The reason is that a quantum computer will be infinitely faster than today's machines and they will be able to break the cryptography used to secure Bitcoin and all other cryptocurrencies, just like how Alan Turing's analogue computer broke the Nazi Enigma machine with unbelievable speed compared to a human. However, there are many developers and researchers already working on ways to protect Bitcoin from this very threat. Quantum computers may not be with us for several decades yet, so this is not something to be concerned with just now.

Taxation and regulation in the US (and to a much lesser extent the UK) has been a growing issue with Bitcoin for some time. It seems various governments across the world were slow to react to Bitcoin but are now slowly starting to make life difficult for companies and even regular users. This uncertainty and lack of clarity is starting to annoy some people and worry others. Over the years in the US at least, each different government agency who has any clout or interest in the matter has labelled bitcoin as a different type of asset.[18] The lack of clarity the world over is spreading doubt to some degree on how Bitcoin can be adopted, but it is important to note that many companies in the space along with wealthy individuals are working tirelessly with their staff and legal counsel, to work with and guide the regulators and politicians to sensible solutions. There are also several notable organisations and think tanks within the space who are working closely with, and lobbying the politicians to make sure any regulations set in place are fair and legal, such as CryptoUk, Digital Currency Group and Coin Centre. Another important point to consider is that with every passing quarter, more and more wealthy individuals, policymakers and politicians are buying their first bitcoin, meaning *they* do not want to upset the apple cart too much and destroy the future growth of their new digital asset.

Another negative side of the regulation is how regulators are forcing the exchanges to comply with various stipulations. Most exchanges need to collect identifiable information on their users, such as their name and postal address, when you first open an account with them. This is so they can comply with banking regulations and the two big laws within that known as AML and KYC (Anti-Money Laundering and Know Your

---

[18] The CFTC (Commodities Futures Trading Commission) for example, has designated bitcoin as a commodity, while the IRS (Internal Revenue Service, the US version of HMRC in the UK) treats it as property and therefore it is taxed accordingly under their jurisdiction. While FinCEN deems bitcoin virtual currency. Different US state regulators claim it to be a currency while a court in Florida has passed their judgement stating it is not a currency. In the UK it is largely unregulated (aside from AML and KYC banking regulations) and is not regarded as legal tender but is labelled more as a foreign/private currency. It is subject to capital gains tax and in some cases VAT. This uncertainty highlights how individuals in the space need to research their own governments' regulations and act accordingly.

Customer respectively) this has been happening for a few years now and was a necessary evil. Now, however, the regulators are making the exchanges monitor the Bitcoin addresses involved with customer deposits and withdrawals (and even the addresses one or two hops in front of the deposit and beyond the withdrawal). If a bitcoin transaction comes from or goes to a 'suspicious' address then this needs to be flagged and reported. This has worried many Bitcoiners massively, as not only does it infringe on people's rights and to some extent punch the ethics of Bitcoin square in the face, it sets a very worrying precedent for certain bitcoin to become tainted or blacklisted and to not be equal to other bitcoin. This starts to erode bitcoin's fungibility. Being fungible means they are replaceable by another identical item, to be mutually interchangeable. Just as a kilo of pure gold is no different from any other kilo of pure gold.

In the realm of cash, this argument was tested in the mid-1700s.[19] As a workaround, along with an effective way of trying to protect their privacy, many Bitcoiners utilise a service from separate technologies known as a CoinJoin, CoinMixers and Coin Tumblers. This is where individuals group their coins into a pool, which gets mixed and returns different coins to all the participants. This confuses the agencies and analytics companies who are monitoring certain coins/addresses; however, the regulators are now starting to put pressure on exchanges who accept deposits from a CoinJoin. Many Bitcoin developers are working on making these mixing services more mainstream. It would appear there is a race on between the developers and

---

[19] When a Scottish judge deemed that a previously stolen banknote that finally found its way back into a bank vault, (long after the robber spent it) was no longer the legal property of the former owner, who had noted the serial number and even signed his name on the note. As the judge put it, if merchants across Scotland had to scour through newspapers to check the legitimacy of every banknote they receive to check it hasn't been stolen, then the country would grind to a halt and the financial system would become unworkable.

regulators to nip the issue in the bud. The regulators wish for a world where all bitcoin transactions are monitored, including the mapping of the history of each individual coins use, while many developers are quickly trying to insert privacy leaning protocols into the Bitcoin software or at very least the apps that we all use. Many staunch advocates of Bitcoin privacy are calling for us all to use these mixing services, so that if a high percentage of all bitcoin become 'tainted' by this process, they believe the regulators will have to drop the matter.

As I have said already, it is unclear how Bitcoin will develop, evolve, and become adopted by people. This great experiment may fizzle out, or it could morph into something different with an even newer technology taking the limelight away from cryptocurrency and blockchains. Or a new or already existing crypto could overtake Bitcoin and become universally adopted and settle as the world's de facto cryptocurrency. The Bitcoin developers, miners and users could all disagree on how it should evolve, and this could easily fracture Bitcoin into varying versions. We could end up with Bitcoin Cash, along with other forks of Bitcoin. One that becomes the extra private version, one used for day to day purchases, and another used as a store of value. The regulators and governments of the world could throw a spanner into the works and derail Bitcoin, or a multitude of other scenarios could surface. Modern fiat currencies are a little over 100 years old, Bitcoin is much younger, and it is very unclear how this new economy will mature. I only thought it was best to add this chapter to show the reader that anything can happen and that no pundit out there has a crystal ball that they are consulting with. That being said, millions of users feel that Bitcoin is here for the long term and that mass adoption is just around the corner.

IS BITCOIN MINING BAD FOR
THE ENVIRONMENT?

This subject could have easily been placed in the previous chapter, as many people see this as a *very* negative and hugely unnecessary aspect of Bitcoin. However, it is quite a large topic, and for this reason, I thought it warranted its own chapter. Many people site that Bitcoin mining is unhealthy for the environment, (as the energy used globally by the miners can be compared to the electricity usage of a small country) and some cry out "Bitcoin is boiling the oceans"! According to an article on www.digiconomist.net they compare Bitcoin's annualized carbon footprint to that of Denmark. Its electrical consumption to Austria and its electronic waste as being the same as Luxembourg. They go one further and even add that the carbon footprint of a *single* bitcoin transaction is comparable to the carbon footprint of 731,850 Visa transactions or 48,790 hours of watching YouTube. These are awfully specific numbers; I wonder how accurate they are. In all industries and areas of life, there is fake news and FUD, (see Appendix A) making it hard for anyone to determine what is real or not. I am not suggesting this to be the case with the above article and their figures, but I imagine there is lots and lots of fiat currency greasing palms and lots of lobbying of governments and policymakers with regards to discrediting and trying to quash Bitcoin and cryptocurrency in general. Why? Because it threatens the status quo of the establishment, the establishment that has had a pretty nice and firm grip on the financial strings that the whole world relies on.

These reports on energy usage may be true; however, I wonder how much energy is used by the traditional banking sector and all the associated companies globally. How many server rooms do all the banks have dotted around the planet? How many tens of millions of square feet in office space is being kept warm or cold for staff? How many fluorescent bulbs or LEDs are used to light the banks, offices, and server rooms? What are the construction *and* environmental costs of the plush skyscrapers that all the large banking firms have these days? Then you could consider how much energy is spent in printing the currency we handle, or the energy used and the environmental impact of our plastic bank cards and the new polypropylene banknotes. Or all the associated costs to grow the cotton used globally in the older generation of banknotes, not to forget the ink and electricity to print them. Next consider the diesel used by security staff to drive the currency to and from the banks, shops and the ATMs across the whole world! While we are there, do not forget to include the millions upon millions of litres of fuel used annually by *all* the bank staff commuting to and from their places of work. How about including the combined wages of all the bank staff, including the executives with their hefty bonuses. The real cost of our financial system must be enormous, most of which we, the customers absorb. Is it conceivable that cryptocurrencies could work out more cost-effective and maybe even greener if someone were able to perform the complex calculations required?

According to an article on www.newsbtc.com in 2018 alone, the US government produced 7.4 billion banknotes, at a cost of:

- $800 million to manufacture the notes.
- $24 million to transport.
- $14 million to conduct quality assurance.
- $7 million for counterfeit deterrence.

Remember these figures only relate to the 2018 production and do not include all the associated costs of supporting and managing the already existing supply.

They also reported that there are an estimated $3 billion in counterfeit notes globally and that Bitcoin has zero counterfeit coins...oh and that Bitcoin also costs the taxpayer nothing.

In contrast to the doom and gloom that most articles bring regarding Bitcoin's energy usage, there was a refreshing report released from the cryptocurrency asset management and analysis firm CoinShares. Their report states that most of the electricity used by Bitcoin comes from clean sources, like wind, solar and hydropower. They say the Bitcoin network gets as much as 74% of its electricity from renewables, making it 'more renewables-driven then almost any other large-scale industry in the world'. Their report also points to a broader problem of how renewable energy is currently deployed around the world with many renewable power generators being underused and poorly located. So much so, that Bitcoin mining has become the only viable use for that energy and that if Bitcoin miners did not utilise it then the electricity would go to waste. Other analysts are sceptical of this report, so the mystery of how good or bad Bitcoin's energy usage has become is left unsolved for the moment.

For those of you interested in hearing a famous Bitcoin educator explaining his thoughts on Bitcoin's power usage, you can search YouTube for the following: Bitcoin Q&A: Energy consumption and you will find a 5:51 video of Andreas M. Antonopoulos speaking about Bitcoin mining, and how it may be possible to describe Bitcoin as actually being green, and how the world could well need at least one, power-intensive, proof of work cryptocurrency like Bitcoin. Now we have exhausted all the negative news I have, let's now continue to learn positive information about this new technology.

HOW ADOPTION MIGHT GROW

Cryptocurrency is here to stay; it can't be uninvented. How it will develop and integrate itself with the current system and our day-to-day lives is still unknown. Which cryptocurrency will prevail as the most dominant is anyone's guess. How the various top-performing cryptos will interact and co-exist is still unclear. However, crypto adoption is growing, and large scale business and institutional developments are starting to build behind the scenes in a big way. At the end of this book I shall show you a few of the recent crypto news headlines that for one reason or another, the mainstream media is not reporting. Have they been asked to keep quiet on the subject and at best only report on the negative headlines? With any new technology, it can take time for adoption to kick in.[20] Looking at the stats on Television adoption, which was invented in 1927, we have learnt that by the end of the 1940s only 2% of American families owned a TV. Email was invented in 1972 and yet it took 15 years to pass the 10 million user count.

Andreas and other influencers in the space understand that for Westerners, Bitcoin is not a necessity right now. The interest in the developed world is more speculative, whereas it is the rest of the world that desperately needs a system like Bitcoin. In his words, Bitcoin is here to bank the unbanked (people with no bank account). The World Bank reports that roughly 2 billion people are unbanked. Many believe this figure is calculated incorrectly and that the true figure is much higher.

---

[20] With regards to smartphones, not everyone bought an iPhone when they were first invented, it took time for the benefits of this new technology to propagate. Some of us waited for the second or third generation so that any bugs could be ironed out. Others waited until Samsung released even cheaper models; while some people in the Western world only recently got their first smartphone, twelve years after the first one was released.

The figure for the underbanked (people with insufficient access to banking) could be as high as 6 billion! Looking at Africa for example, we can only speculate how adoption might grow there. It is interesting to notice how their telecommunications network has evolved. They leapfrogged the need for traditional copper wired telephone lines over most of the continent and jumped straight into using mobile technology. They have now circumnavigated the need for the older system and are quickly adopting mobile phones. Will Africa and all the other underserviced and impoverished populations the world over, repeat this move with the financial system that they've never truly had? Will they leapfrog again and adopt cryptocurrency, the newer, faster, and fairer way of storing and sending value to each other? Many countries in South America are starting to adopt Bitcoin and other cryptocurrencies quite readily.

Many countries around the world have financial systems much worse than our own, with some currencies inflating at unbelievable speeds. Venezuela is a modern and extreme example of a country in economic ruin. Their hyperinflation is soon expected to hit 10,000,000% which pushes the price of everything up unbelievably fast. Merchants are having to change the price of their good's multiple times a day just to keep up with their hyperinflation. While many workers across the country are given a new hourly rate at lunchtime (each day) to reflect the constantly devaluing currency! As a result of this, an estimated 5 million Venezuelans have left the country to seek a better life. This includes a substantial amount of 'brain drain'.[21]

All this turmoil makes the need for a fairer and potentially more

---

[21] Where the educated families and prospective college and university students leave a failing country to seek better employment/education. This only makes matters worse for the country in question, as they lose many of the current and future teachers, engineers, inventors, politicians and so on.

stable currency like bitcoin, all the more important for these struggling nations.

According to an article on bitcoinist.com, bitcoin is now the 8th largest world currency, ranking it larger than Russia, South Korea, Brazil, Canada and Norway. Should bitcoin's price continue to rise, it will soon overtake the likes of India, Switzerland, and the UK and then only the comparative giants of Japan, the Eurozone, China and the USA will remain.

Below is an illustration showing the *Adoption Bell Curve* which details how new technologies are adopted by the public.

You can see the initial slight growth that is first experienced as the innovators test a new technology. Then the steady rise as the early adopters enter the space, followed by the steep climb as most of the public rush in. The tailing off follows as most people have already adopted the tech and all that remain are the people who are slow to adopt any new technology. It is believed that we are currently still in the early adopter phase (however the reader should note that Bitcoin may not follow this curve perfectly or even at all, as currently, we do not know if true adoption will take place. This curve may only become accurate after the fact or once we at least hit the zenith in a few more years).

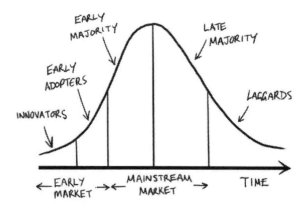

CRYPTO EXCHANGES

There are many different cryptocurrency exchanges on the internet. There are possibly hundreds now dotted around the world, all having different coins available along with different trading volumes. These exchanges can be broken into three basic types.

- <u>Fiat to crypto.</u> Exchanges that enable you to enter fiat currency and exchange it for cryptocurrency and vice versa. Use your pounds, dollars, or euros to buy bitcoin. In this book, I recommend people use the exchange Kraken. They have served the community for many years, have good security and low fees.

- <u>Crypto to crypto.</u> These exchanges only allow for crypto to crypto trading (no fiat government currency allowed). For example, here you could buy VeChain with your newly acquired bitcoin. For this service, I recommend the exchange called Binance.

- <u>Decentralised.</u> The latest generation is known as a decentralised exchange (DEX). Here you can trade crypto to crypto directly with other individuals and no trust is needed as your crypto and keys are always held by yourself.

Fiat to crypto exchanges

Everyone must use the first type of exchange. It is here that people can buy their first bitcoin using British pounds, euros or dollars. Due to various regulatory requirements, all of the large exchanges will need you to prove your identity before they can allow you to register an account with them. This will usually include a scan of your passport or driving licence along with proof of residence. Once this is complete you will be all set. Kraken is a highly regulated exchange, meaning it's as safe as it gets for beginners wanting to buy bitcoin. Kraken also allows its members to buy a fair selection of the top coins available, these include:

- Bitcoin
- Ethereum
- Litecoin
- Basic Attention Token
- Monero
- Tron
- Dash
- EOS
- Stellar Lumens
- XRP
- Zcash
- Lisk
- DAI
- USDC
- Omesigo

Some other regulated and well-known exchanges (should you not want to use Kraken) include Bitstamp, LocalBitcoins and Coinbase.[22] Kraken allows users to buy bitcoin and a large selection of the top altcoins and has low trading fees.

---

[22] The number of alternative coins available on Bitstamp and LocalBitcoins is limited compared to Kraken. Coinbase is a beginner-friendly exchange, however, the trade-off here is that their fees are considered by many to be quite high. Many people are also unhappy with Coinbase as they appear to sell user information to governments quite readily.

Remember using an exchange like Kraken, is the way to get your foot in the crypto door to start with. Once you have some bitcoin you can then progress to the second type of exchange. Following this link will support me in my mission and take you to Kraken to open your account. https://r.kraken.com/L6oRV Appendix B at the end of this book has a walkthrough guide detailing how to open an account with Kraken along with how to use their site to buy your first bitcoin. It is a valuable guide for people wishing to join the new economy.

Crypto to crypto exchanges

Should you wish to buy or trade the multitude of other cryptocurrencies available, you will need to join the next category of exchanges, the type that handles crypto to crypto trading. Binance is a popular crypto to crypto exchange that will serve your needs should you wish to buy most of the popular cryptocurrencies. They have 150 available and are also geared up for active trading, with colourful trading charts and analysis tools.[23] This chapter has only covered how to purchase crypto. However, if you wish to try your hand at crypto trading, exchanges like Binance will be the place to do it. Be warned though, as sharks are circling out there in the warm crypto waters! Time-served veterans, some of whom have migrated over from the forex trading platforms, so take heed of the advice that you should only trade with currency you are comfortable loosing.

---

[23] If a reader wishes to trade currency pairs, some familiarisation of these systems would be greatly advised before a beginner jumps in headfirst. It is important to note that speculative trading is a different kettle of fish compared to simply buying bitcoin on Kraken and then if you wish, using this bitcoin to buy your chosen coin on Binance! Further learning should be carried out if you wish to actively trade currency pairs, as is traditionally done in the foreign exchange (forex) markets.

Following this link https://www.binance.com/?ref=11033695 will take you to Binance.

Decentralised exchanges

The third type is the DEX, the decentralised exchange and these are still on the drawing boards being designed. This new generation of exchange endeavours to provide a platform where people trade peer to peer, directly between themselves, where funds are never held on the exchange itself. As the funds are not held on the exchange, this means the exchange operators do not hold your private keys. For this reason, a DEX will be the safest way that people can trade crypto in the future. The DEX will become the future of cryptocurrency exchanges, but they will not be ready to receive new customers for some time yet.

The steps required to purchase bitcoin

To clarify, I will detail the process I have recommended to my family and friends, should they wish to enter the space.

- I would tell them to firstly open an account with Kraken. Here they can transfer fiat currency directly from their bank to their Kraken account and use it to buy themselves some bitcoin. Keeping their new bitcoin on Kraken is very safe and is more than acceptable until they are ready to progress to the next level of custody and hold the bitcoin themselves.

- Then if they wished to expand their crypto holdings, I would recommend they join the exchange Binance. They can transfer a small portion of their bitcoin from Kraken to Binance. Then the whole world is their oyster and they will have access to over 150 different cryptocurrencies and digital tokens on the Binance exchange.

- I would then ask them to strongly consider buying a Ledger Nano X so they can safely store their bitcoin and various altcoins on their own. As to solely rely on these exchanges (even though they are both highly regarded), is not best practice and is not why we are here. Many people enter the crypto world to become their own bank and store their keys and coins by themselves.

- The Capsule from the company Cryptosteel would be the next product I would recommend to a new Bitcoiner. The device will protect their seed phrase for a lifetime, in their words offering; 'The mother of all backups'.

- Kraken, Binance, Ledger and Cryptosteel are the four companies that will allow you to enter the crypto world safely and become your own bank. At my website, I have links to join both exchanges and I also have a link for the Ledger Nano X and Capsule.
  https://www.thebitcoinbook.co.uk

Although I have mentioned this previously it bears repeating. When you use the services of an exchange, you are trusting them to keep your crypto (your private keys) safe, and the exchange operator will be the legal custodians of your assets (except in the case of a future DEX). They will hold your private keys and could theoretically lose your funds should they be attacked. Kraken, Binance and many of the top exchanges out there are extremely safe, but even so, best practice is to aim to secure your digital assets yourself. Unless you are actively trading cryptocurrencies, it is not best practice to leave your digital assets on the exchanges, especially for the long term. People should move it to wallets that they control, such as a PC or hardware wallet.

There are not many exchanges in this space who have not been hacked. Even the exchange Binance, that I recommend in this book has been hacked. This was to the tune of 7,000 bitcoin

(£31 million at the time). Even though this sounds quite worrying, Binance has been praised since their inception as being a market leader in the space. Long before they were hacked they started to set aside a portion of their trading fees, and have built up a handsome kitty that could be used to reimburse customers should they ever be hacked.

Well, unfortunately, that day came for Binance. They are not 100% sure how the hack happened but believe that it was customers passwords that were compromised and not a security weakness on their exchange. Either way, it is reassuring that Binance refunded their customers and I'm sure they will continue to be one of the top-ranked crypto exchanges for some time to come. That is why I am still more than happy to recommend Binance and their services.

Not all exchanges operate with high morals and openness and to highlight this and finish this chapter, I will briefly touch on two famous stories, one is old, and the other is happening as I write. They both show the need for individuals in the space to recognise the importance of storing your private keys, and only holding small amounts of cryptocurrency on exchanges.

The first story is from way back in 2014 and focuses on the exchange Mt. Gox (*Magic the Gathering Online Exchange*). It is the story of how an exchange owner lost most of the customers bitcoin he was holding. Based in Japan, Mt. Gox was one of the world's first bitcoin exchanges. Business was booming until (for reasons still unknown to this day) they became insolvent. Meaning they did not hold all the bitcoin they should have been. They limited withdrawals and then stopped them altogether. When the dust settled and after Japanese law enforcement had raided the offices, the extent of the damage was fully realised. Over 850,000 bitcoin were unaccounted for! 200,000 were then found, but the company was forced into receivership and a slow legal battle ensued. There have been many attempts to retrieve the lost bitcoin, or at least refund the customers. With the case still far from being closed, the saga still hits the crypto headlines from time to time. The last news I heard on this story was that some wealthy individuals in the space are attempting to relaunch the exchange and that the reimbursement of many of the former customers is soon to take place.

Another mind-boggling story is from the Canadian exchange called QuadrigaCX. For some unknown reason, the CEO of this exchange, Gerald Cotton, was the only person who had access to the private keys for *all* customer deposits. There were no back-ups of the private keys to customer wallets, no third party involvement with regards to security or the use of multisig.[24] With no backups, Cotton travelled to India to do some charity work where he died from complications of Crone's disease. Now the exchange staff are left scratching their heads as the now-deceased CEO has taken the private keys to the grave with him! The staff and customers are now locked out of the customer's crypto wallets to the tune of $250 million. The plot thickens, as it is believed he updated his will two weeks before his death. The most worrying concern is that people have started to investigate the various blockchains involved and they believe that some of the coins within the locked wallets are moving. Many people believe the CEO is not dead and has executed an exit scam, where everything operates normally and then one day the perpetrator flees with people's investments. Some people believe the Mafia was using his exchange to launder money and through bad practices, Cotton lost most or all of their cash, which is estimated to be in the tens of millions. I guess this would be a good enough reason to fake your own death and go into hiding, as this is the last group of people you would want to upset. The FBI and RCMP of Canada are heavily

---

[24] Multisig stands for multiple signatures. It is a security feature which gives multiple people their own private key for the same crypto address. A specified ratio of these people are needed to sign a transaction for it to become valid and to be broadcast on the network. We shall briefly look at multisig again in the security chapter, as it is a good way for people, families, and businesses to protect themselves.

investigating this crime, and it is believed some of the claimants will be paid back a percentage of their losses through money and investments that have been seized from the Cotton estate, and that they may even try to exhume the body to check if there has been any foul play.

THE DIFFERENT TYPES OF DIGITAL ASSETS

There are several different types of coins or tokens available. In this chapter, we shall see how they can be designated. Before we do, let's quickly look at how some coins can be launched. In 2017, a new way of releasing a coin was established, called an Initial Coin Offering (ICO). This is just a fancy new term for a pre-sale. This new approach on how to release a digital asset to market took the crypto world by storm. Many companies who released a 'coin' using this model, branded their coin a 'utility token' and not a currency. This meant that if you bought their token now, before their company or product was even established/produced, you would have the ability to use this to interact with their future business, to spend the token for their goods and services.

However, many people *were* buying these tokens/digital assets not for their intended future use, but solely for investment purposes, believing the price would rise and in the future, they could make a decent return on their investment. The phrase token was used to avoid the attention of the financial regulators.[25] The regulators were unsure if the companies releasing their coins under this ICO model were illegally selling a security (a financial product, where a profit can be expected) or a legitimate token, so they had to take a closer look.

Since that time the American regulators have come forward with a negative view of the whole ICO/token phenomenon and have started to investigate many companies that used the ICO model to release their cryptocurrency, to see if there has been any lawbreaking.

---

[25] Such as the SEC *(Securities Exchange Commission)* in America and the FCA *(Financial Conduct Authority)* in the UK, as it is illegal for companies to release a financial product, where profits are expected, if the issuing company doesn't have a securities licence.

Bitcoin and ether have been deemed by the American regulators to *not* be securities and are therefore at the top of the list of safe cryptocurrencies that the regulators will not investigate further. This cannot be said for many of the other cryptocurrencies available. We will look a little closer at ICOs shortly. For now, let's look at the various types of digital assets available and see how they are categorised. Remember that not all the cryptocurrencies available are designed to be used as money. The shortlist below designates them into an easily understandable category.

Cryptocurrency: A currency or digital asset that is used for daily trade, like pounds and dollars or is used to store value, like gold.

Privacy coins: Again, used for general trade or as a store of value, but these coins have been specially designed with privacy in mind. Bitcoin and many other cryptocurrencies are private to some extent, but users are not completely anonymous. Whereas some of these newer generation of coins have been designed in such a way as to be as private as possible, with some claiming to have zero traceability on their blockchains.

Stablecoins: These coins are backed by an actual pound/euro/dollar stored in the issuing companies bank account. A bit like how the *old* pound and dollar used to be backed by an ounce of gold. The company that releases a Stablecoin, should only release one coin for every unit of fiat currency held in their bank, and because of this reason, the Stablecoin's price will stay fixed to the fiat currency that backs it. As most Stablecoins have been released by American companies they are priced at $1. They may fluctuate ever so slightly, but only by a cent or two. One TUSD *Trust United States Dollar* is a Stablecoin released by the company Trust Token. They have recently released a Trust Stablecoin for the British pound. It is called TGBP *Trust Great British Pound*, along with one for Europe and another for China. These coins are designed to be a lot more price stable than your average cryptocurrency.

They are used to protect people from price volatility, the fluctuations in price that bitcoin and other cryptos experience. For various reasons, a person may wish to sell their bitcoin and store its value in a Stablecoin. Doing so would effectively lock in their crypto holdings at that price point. Any big swing, up or down, in the bitcoin price, would then not affect their position. Using an exchange they could 'cash out' of the Stablecoin into their national fiat currency or repurchase bitcoin once the volatility has stabilised. There are several Stablecoins available at present, with a couple being launched by some of the big exchanges. I thought it prudent to mention that many people in the community believe that Tether, the company behind the Stablecoin USDT, may not be operating fully above board. Are they being a little shady with proving how many dollars they are holding in their bank account? Tether and their coin USDT should not be confused with the first Stablecoin I mentioned in this section from Trust Token, TUSD. Having said that, Tether (USDT) is the most widely traded cryptocurrency in the market, beating bitcoin and all other cryptocurrencies in trading volume. However, remember Tether and all other Stablecoins are designed to always be worth only $1/£1 and will *never* climb in price as bitcoin has.

Utility tokens: Not strictly speaking a currency, but an asset that allows the owner to purchase a specific company's products or services. As a made-up example, we could imagine a token called 'King & Queen Coffee'. Holders of this fictitious token can use the KQC token to pay for all the products and services that the chain of King & Queen Coffee shops sell. This is the type of cryptocurrency that the regulators are showing an interest in. As they believe many small investors have purchased coins like this, not necessarily for its intended future use, but because of their own (or the issuing company's) belief that it will be valued much higher in the future.

Some companies offering tokens like this fictitious one may have illegally promoted financial gains to uneducated investors.

Security tokens: A new type of token designed specifically to be regulator friendly and to allow companies to sell securities (financial products) to investors. We will look closer at these new tokens in another chapter.

DApp platforms: Money was the first application that Satoshi designed Bitcoin and blockchains to be used for. Other information can also be transacted, stored and managed on blockchains. Now, all these years later, new ways of using and interacting with blockchains are being realised and developed. Two new use cases are DApps and smart contracts. These technologies, just like cryptocurrency could well become second nature to us all in the coming years. Just as there is a race to become the most excepted cryptocurrency, there are also many companies fighting to become the go-to platform to develop these decentralised applications and smart contracts.

Non-Fungible Tokens: (NFT) Also known as a nifty. These tokens are not mutually interchangeable like bitcoin. They are designed to be limited and individual. Popular uses for these types of tokens have been in the collectable trading card, gaming and art world. Game designers are now able to make NFT's into all manner of in-game assets, such as achievement badges, in-game weapons, 'skins' for weaponry, clothing and potions, anything that can be added into a game. These NFTs are then controlled by the gamer and not the game company. If a player is awarded one or buys one, they can use this token/asset within the game they are playing and even sell them outside the game environment on a third-party marketplace. One famous use for these NFTs was the 2017 hit called CryptoKitties. Here people could purchase these rare virtual cats and even breed them to make other cats. In 2017 one cat reportedly sold for $117,000. With the ability for these tokens to be designed in such a way, so that they are limited, it has allowed collectable card manufacturers and artists to limit their productions, or even to make (cryptographically verifiable) one-offs.

Central Bank Digital Currency: (CBDC) Inspired by Bitcoin, over 40 central banks around the world are interested in the possibilities that releasing their own fiat currency in the form of a digital asset could bring. How this will be done is unclear at this time however, many report that they will not utilise an open blockchain. Personally, I do not know a great deal about this development, or how it will be implemented, but am sceptical of these banks and do not assume that it will be a great development for the end-user. I imagine it will simply give the issuing body even greater control over the people who use the new currency. I much prefer the thought of using an open and fair, non-inflatable cryptocurrency like Bitcoin! China seems to be leading the charge and has been talking of releasing their own for a few years now.

TOP COINS EXPLAINED

In this chapter, we will look at the specific uses and stats of some of the top coins available. One important point to note is that not all cryptocurrencies are decentralised like bitcoin. Many other coins are managed by individuals, or companies, while others are run via trusts. Some have CEOs and offices, while others are managed similarly to Bitcoin, with no one person in control. There are pros and cons to each approach, but it is important to note how a cryptocurrency is structured. Bitcoin is special for many reasons; however, not all the coins that followed have copied Bitcoin's principles, structure, or any of its many attributes. Figures will be rounded to the nearest whole number. Please note that due to cryptocurrency fundamentals and the delay between writing and your reading, circulating supplies will have undoubtedly changed.

This chapter's focus will primarily be on the coins use and circulating/total supplies and will not include their price, as these fluctuate daily.

<u>Bitcoin/BTC</u>: The Grandfather of all cryptocurrencies.

Used for: Currency/Store of value.
Current supply: 18.3 million.
Total supply: 21 million.

<u>Ether/ETH</u>: The first cryptocurrency for creating DApps and smart contracts. Many of the 3,000 cryptocurrencies and digital tokens available are Ethereum based tokens, known as ERC20 tokens, meaning they are used on the Ethereum blockchain. Ethereum was Co-invented by Vitalik Burterin who was a teenager at the time. He originally wanted his idea for decentralised apps and smart contracts to be developed on the Bitcoin blockchain, but the BTC developers were reluctant to make the changes to the code that was required. This frustrated the young developer, so he created his own blockchain.

Used for: It is not a currency per se; however, I am sure some people use it so. Some people make the analogy that if bitcoin is digital gold then ether is digital oil, as ether is the digital asset that 'powers' the Ethereum blockchain and its DApp/smart contract platform. If you want to develop your own app to run on the Ethereum network you need to use ether to pay for this capability. New ways of interacting with blockchains are now being realised, and Ethereum was the first to lead the way. You will shortly discover many other cryptocurrencies in this list are following this model, with many believing their approach will be more successful. This new use for blockchain tech could radically transform many industries especially disrupting the legal sector. Imagine a future where you sell your house for bitcoin. Your proof of ownership and your house deeds are held on the Bitcoin or Ethereum blockchain and you sell your home to an individual using an Ethereum Smart Contract. No solicitors, estate agents or even a bank required. Bliss! Current supply: 110 million.
Total supply: Not currently set.

XRP: Formally (and still occasionally) called Ripple by some people, it was released by the company Ripple Labs.
Its primarily focused on gaining institutional users such as banks to use it for their inter-bank settlements. Because of this reason, the company are not marketing XRP towards the public per se, although the public can buy the coin and speculate on its price. As there is such a large supply of XRP it will never rise in price like bitcoin has and (in my opinion) will only ever reach double digits, or triple at absolute best. The large American bank J.P. Morgan Chase released their own competitor to this coin, called JPM coin, which might massively hinder the adoption of XRP.
Used for: Inter-bank currency.
Current supply: 44 billion.
Total supply: 100 billion.

Litecoin/LTC: This coin was created in 2011 by Charlie Lee who is lovingly nicknamed Satoshi Lite by the crypto community. It is sited as being the silver to 'bitcoin's gold'. When the crypto space was still young, many users believed bitcoin would be used for larger value purchases, or as a store of value, whereas litecoin would be used more like cash and would be used for everyday smaller purchases. Litecoin is designed to have four times as many coins than bitcoin and to also be four times faster. Its block time is 2.5 minutes to Bitcoin's 10 minute blocks. Lee was recently criticised when he announced that he had sold the majority of his litecoin. He says he did this so that he could focus on developing the coin and not be swayed or distracted by the price. Litecoin has an almost symbiotic relationship with bitcoin, as some developments to the Bitcoin code are occasionally tested on the smaller coins blockchain first. It is quite possible in the future that the two coins could coexist and thrive together.

Used for: Currency.

Current supply: 64.3 million.

Total supply: 84 million.

EOS: This is a platform striving to compete with Ethereum. The competition will be high in the DApps/smart contract sector. The developer of this coin has already launched two other coins. He believes that his new platform will not experience the growing pains that Ethereum is encountering and that it will have much higher transactional capabilities. One criticism of EOS is that it is not as decentralised as BTC or ETH, who both have tens of thousands of miners. Whereas EOS has a panel of 21 elected block producers who manage their network. The block producers (who are generally spread around the planet) are periodically voted in and out by the EOS community. Great things have been expected from this project, as their claims were high and so was the funding. The project had a yearlong ICO (Initial Coin Offering), where they made $4.1 billion. The community are a little frustrated at the rate of development and some believe the project has already hit obstacles that they cannot overcome. The 21 elected block producer model, along with other factors may have proved to be extremely costly for the project and the coming year or so may reveal if EOS is to survive for the long term or not.

Used for: DApps/smart contracts.

Current supply: 921 million.

Total supply: 1 billion.

Binance Token/BNB: This token is used by people who have accounts with the popular cryptocurrency exchange Binance. By holding BNB in your Binance account, you can use this token to pay your trading fees (at a reduced rate) as opposed to being charged a small percentage of the coin you are trading. If you intend to purchase any of the cryptocurrencies in the wider market I recommend you look at using the Binance exchange. They are a trusted exchange who have trail blazed for the community. If you intend to buy, and especially if you wish to trade multiple cryptocurrencies, you could look at buying a small amount of their BNB token as it will allow you to lower your trading fees. The BNB token is one of the few cryptographic assets that a staunch Bitcoin maximalist can see a credible use for.

Used for: Reducing trading fees.

Current supply: 155 million.

Total supply: 187 million.

Stellar Lumens/XLM: The organisation Stellar is attempting to compete with the likes of PayPal and Western Union. It is creating a global network where currency can be exchanged quickly between individuals. Fees are low, and the transactions are very fast. Their currency is called Lumens, although many people refer to them as Stellar. It is a fork of XRP, and its team is made up of former Ripple Labs employees.

In 2019 the Stellar Development Foundation purposefully destroyed 55 billion XLM to lower the overall supply. This is called 'burning' and is done by sending the coins to an address with no private keys, meaning once they are sent to the 'burn address' they can no longer be used and are effectively destroyed. These coins were held by the Stella Foundation and had not yet been released into the general market.
Used for: Currency.
Current supply: 20.2 billion.
Total supply: 50 billion.

Cardano/ADA: This coin is a merger of both a cryptocurrency and a DApp/smart contract platform. It is being developed globally by academics and engineers. It is considerably younger than many of the other projects out there, but it quickly found itself in the top 20 when ranked by its market cap.
Used for: Currency, DApps and smart contracts.
Current supply: 26 billion.
Total supply: 31 billion.

Monero/XMR: The highest capped privacy coin. Argued by many to be the most private of all the privacy coins. Monero transactions are much more private than Bitcoin. This is another coin that many Bitcoiners also seem to like.
Used for: Currency.
Current supply: 17.5 million.
Total supply: Unclear, as once 18.4 million are in circulation, 0.3 XMR will be produced every minute, forever.

Tron/TRX: The team behind Tron is hoping to make a decentralised entertainment ecosystem and DApp/smart contract platform. They claim their system has much more transactional capabilities compared to Ethereum and boast a high number of DApps already, many in the gambling and gaming sectors. Tron recently purchased the famous file sharing platform BitTorrent for over $100 million and have also released a crypto token within BitTorrent called BTT. They sold 50 million BTT tokens in just 15 minutes during its ICO! With BitTorrent spread around 138 countries and users clocking in at over 100 million, it looks like both TRX and BTT will bring lots of attention to the benefits of blockchain technology. Many pundits don't like Tron believing it is just a fly-by-night project and not a very serious one at that, however it seems that it could be here for the long run and it is slowly proving to some people that its goals are serious and it intends to stay and make its mark.

Used for: Service interaction.

Current supply: 66.7 billion.

Total supply: 99.3 billion.

As you can see from this chapter, many of these coins have total supplies that vary from Bitcoin. Remember also, that just because a coin is very cheap, it does not necessarily mean it will climb in value as bitcoin has. It may have different fundamentals and a much larger supply, meaning it is not as scarce as bitcoin is. Search the subject *Unit Bias* for more information on this. One important fact you might like to know is that at the point of creation, a development team can decide how these coins are to be released. In the case of bitcoin, it was slowly mined from the offset with zero being available at the very start and then at the end of the first-ever block (referred to as the genesis block) the first block reward was issued, and the cryptocurrency was then 'live' and the first mined coins were now in circulation. That's how Bitcoin and many other cryptos handle their distribution. As we know Bitcoin has continued on this path since 2009, slowly releasing all of its current supply of 18 million coins to the public. The reader should note that not all coins have followed this seemingly very fair way of doing things and have taken a different approach. There is a term in the space known as a pre-mine.

This is where a development team create a percentage, or even all of their coins at the very start of their coin's life with little to no effort (they are simply produced at the start by the click of a button). The coins are then held back in either a smart contract or in a trust, or some type of organisation, or even by an individual, that then slowly releases the coins to market (normally at a predetermined rate). The coin XRP for example, pre-mined all its 100 billion coins on day one, and then every month, they sell up to one billion of them to the market. Those that are not sold are returned to an escrow account. Pre-mining is not necessarily a bad thing, but many people (especially diehard Bitcoiners) see it as a cheeky way of releasing a coin. According to an article on www.steemit.com 63% of the top 100 coins have been pre-mined. The list includes among many others XRP, XLM, ADA, NEM, IOTA, NEO and TRX. A large amount of the original ether (ETH) was also pre-mined before they conducted their ICO, however, they now are actively mined like bitcoin. For many years, the Ethereum developers have been striving to change their system of generating new coins and wish to move away from proof-of-work and adopt proof-of-stake mining. Many Bitcoiners believe the Ethereum developers are struggling to adapt their network to their intended PoS system and that this could seriously hinder the future of the coin.

WHAT IS AN ICO?

ICO stands for Initial Coin Offering and as mentioned earlier is a pre-sale. This was the crypto phenomenon of 2017 that we touched on briefly, where companies gained capital to start or develop their business by issuing their cryptocurrency to participants. These coins/tokens were predominantly pre-mined and then quickly sold to the public. In the world of traditional stocks, when an already established company 'goes public' they are allowing investors to buy the company's shares, this is known as an IPO (initial public offering). An ICO has flipped that model and is more akin to the modern kick-starter approach to raising capital. It's a bit like the company going onto the TV show *Dragons Den/Shark Tank*. Once they have formulated their business plan and have created their coin/token they can start their ICO. They offer the public the chance to buy these coins, which at this stage are generally very cheap. People purchase these coins with the assumption that once the company starts operating, the coin/token will become useful. Once the ICO is complete and all the coins on offer have been sold, the company can use this capital to further its business development. They can then hire more staff, rent office space, and generally get their business ball rolling. However, some people may have taken part in certain ICOs solely in the hope that the value of the coin would rise and they can sell it for a quick profit (this is why the American regulators are investigating many of these issuing companies, as they believe the companies could have mis-sold the asset to unaccredited investors.[26] Not all coins start their life with an

---

[26] Accredited investors are people that have a net worth of over £850,000/$1,000,000 which does not include their primary home. As these people are quite wealthy, the regulators allow them to take more risks than the rest of us, letting them invest more freely compared to your average person.

ICO (aka token sale) and those that don't are sometimes seen as being more legitimate than others. Bitcoin did not have an ICO, it was just released and naturally and slowly adopted by people.

An important thing to note is that not all the coins created during an ICO (and also a pre-mine) need to be issued for general sale. The company may decide to keep a fair percentage of these for themselves. This may simply be for future use, or literally to keep for themselves for their own investment purposes. Or they could be used to pay back even earlier investors, who may have invested before the company was even ready to start the ICO in the first place. There can be legitimate reasons for this, but it is something to be aware of. It is also important to note, that many companies that instigate an ICO may come to nothing. For various reasons, their business might not gain any traction. It should, therefore, be treated as a high-risk investment, or more appropriately, not even as an investment at all but more like a gift for the company, for them to use as they see fit, with no strings attached.

To take part in an ICO, people usually send bitcoin or ether to the company. In return, they will receive an agreed ratio of the company's new cryptocurrency. Most of the recent ICOs have been conducted using ether (the Ethereum blockchains token). The reason for this is that most of these ICO coins are Ethereum based tokens, known as ERC20 tokens. They have been designed to operate on the Ethereum blockchain. Remember that a high percentage of the 3,000 plus cryptocurrencies available are ERC20 tokens. This is an important point to note because if for any reason Ethereum should fail, it could hinder many of these ERC20 tokens. However, many of these projects will be able to move their system and coin to other platforms such as Cardano, Neo, Stella, EOS and Tron. Conversely, if Ethereum does survive for the long term and its developers do upgrade their blockchain from PoW to PoS, because so many of the available coins are ERC20 tokens, it *could* mean ethers price might rise significantly.

Facebook banned crypto advertising, partly due to the ICO craze backfiring for many people. Another reason for the Facebook ban is because they are planning to start their own crypto! Facebook have also been acquiring crypto companies and individuals from the space. We shall briefly discuss Facebook's Libra Coin at the end of this book. For a time, Google also banned crypto advertising, but I believe they have slackened their rules, allowing certain companies to start advertising again. They will most likely not help companies in the future who plan to conduct an ICO, but established and regulated companies will be allowed to advertise on Google.

Once an ICO is complete, the coin will be adopted by the various exchanges who are interested in it. Once live on the open market, anyone who missed out on the ICO can now purchase them. You can expect the price to spike upwards when they initially appear on the exchanges, as people who missed out on the ICO, rush in to buy some of the newly available coins. Many people who invested in the ICO will sell at that point, happy with the financial gains from that initial upward price spike. Many ICO's sell out in minutes or even seconds, with some making hundreds of millions of pounds in that short time. The company Telegram, for example, raised $1.7 billion in early 2018 and at this time still has no product on the market. It has recently been reported that they may be planning to release their own Stablecoin. As mentioned earlier the record goes to EOS who raised a massive $4.1 billion during their year-long ICO. The American regulators did investigate the EOS ICO and reached an agreement in a civil settlement with Block.One, the company behind EOS, and they paid $24 million in fines. It is expected that many ICOs are outright scams, with no intention of actually developing a working business. Most were not scams but were legitimate businesses with every intention to develop their product/coin/business. However, as we know, most businesses fail and now after some bad press, the ICO model may evolve. Many companies having read the writing on the wall, made it purposefully hard for American customers to take part in their ICO (so that the SEC would not investigate them, as Americans were not put at risk). It is possible that once the regulators pass their final judgement on this matter, that the business model will cease to exist, or that future tokens offered in this manner will only be available to accredited investors. Either way, I felt that it was important to include this information for the reader so that they are fully aware of the various ways people can buy coins in the crypto space.

A new approach to the ICO model is that the crypto exchanges themselves have started to conduct the token sale on behalf of the issuing company. This is referred to as an IEO *Initial Exchange Offering,* and it may give the public and regulators a bit more confidence that only credible and vetted companies have passed the exchange's requirements. However, recent reports are that the SEC will start scrutinising some of these businesses, regardless of who operates the release of a coin. These IEO's are in their infancy as only a few have taken place at this time.

INTRODUCING THE STO

In the last chapter, we learnt how the ICO model could cease to exist or that it might morph into something else. If 2017 was the year of the ICO, it must now make way for the new kid on the block, the STO or *Security Token Offering*. This is a new phenomenon and is likely to become the next step in the evolution of cryptocurrencies and digital assets. As mentioned in the last chapter, the regulators had a very dim view of the companies that they believed wrongly sold coins through the ICO model. The industry has now pivoted and designed a regulator friendly digital asset, the Security Token. It is specifically designed to comply with the laws that govern the sale of securities, making it regulator friendly. A security is a financial asset such as stocks or bonds, where the promise of a financial return is expected. The STO model of designing and selling this new generation of digital assets may revolutionise many aspects of finance and investing. It will allow companies to issue their traditional company shares to investors digitally, instead of using the traditional paper or 'electronic' e-share. It will also allow for a new phenomenon to flourish in the digital era, this is called fractional ownership. Maybe not an out-and-out new concept, but new and radical when combined with cryptographically secured digital assets. We are now slowly seeing a future develop where people will be able to use these new types of coins, to invest in fractional ownership of assets such as hotels, sports cars, and even fine art and much more. The new term that also goes side by side with fractional ownership is tokenisation.

In a brief example of this, we can look at an already existing use case where a developer of a new holiday resort, tokenises the entire complex. Meaning that they create a set number of security tokens, where each individual token represents either each suite in the resort (or taken to a more extreme level, a token for every square foot of the holiday complex). These tokens can then be sold to willing investors who will ultimately reap a profit from this ownership, dependant on the number of tokens they hold and the associated profit of the resort. These tokens are designed in such a way that they openly follow the laws that govern the sale of securities, such as who can buy them, how this information is recorded and so forth. Owners of the tokens will be able to easily sell them to other investors on special exchanges. Ownership of the token and even the dividend pay-out itself, could all be theoretically handled by blockchain technology. Many STO platforms are already in operation and are working hard to give their clients the ability to construct and release their own security tokens. That could be for a token to raise business start-up capital, or for issuing existing company shares or tokenising investment properties around the globe. It doesn't stop there, millions of items around us could be tokenised. From luxury cars, holiday homes, fine art, vineyards, and sports stadiums through to a musician's latest album, premiere golf courses and even the raffle tickets for that Victoria sponge cake at the local school's summer fete. Basically, it's all up for grabs! The list of tokenisable items is endless and once perfected by the developers and approved by the regulators, it will undoubtedly become a multi-billion pound industry. Three popular companies who are helping their clients release their own STO are Polymath, Securitize and Swarm.

CRYPTO SECURITY

Many security implications need to be considered when entering the crypto space. I will endeavour to cover as many as I can and focus on the most important ones. This book is only the beginning and you will need to learn a lot, especially with regards to security, if you wish to be as safe as you can. Many people have lost their bitcoin through negligence.

The security advisements below are not in any order. There are many more that you should know, however, I am focusing on the major ones that are the most important for beginners.

This first example is not an out-and-out security issue, but if nothing else shows the need for care when you take the plunge into the warm crypto waters and become your own bank! This famous story is about the Welsh IT worker who mined 7,500 bitcoin! He had mined his BTC a couple of years beforehand and then totally forgot about them. After the 2013 price spike, a news report on the television reminded him that he owned some himself. His heart sank as he then realised that he had only just upgraded the internals of his laptop, having thrown the old hard drive into his black wheelie bin![27] He rushed to the landfill site, to be told roughly where that month's rubbish was dumped but that it was most likely now buried under four feet of additional waste. He and others have spent time trying to find the lost hard drive but to no avail. At the height of the bitcoin price in 2017 that lost hard drive was storing the private keys to approximately £74 million worth of bitcoin. That's a half-decent EuroMillions Lotto win! The last I heard on this story was that he had offered the local council £7.4 million, (10% of the total bounty at the time) if they allowed him to properly dig at the site and should he find the missing hard

---

[27] In 2013 wallets were not backed up as easily as they are today. Back then people had to look after their private key even more thoroughly than they do today. HD wallets and recovery seed phrases did not exist, if they did he would have been able to retrieve access to his bitcoin using his seed phrase, regardless of where his hard drive was buried.

drive *and* be able to recover the bitcoin from the drive. But they were not interested in his offer and have refused his pleas to dig up sections of the landfill. This one-story alone should highlight the need for lots of care when you become your own bank. As a side note, why would a cash strapped council refuse the chance of receiving millions of pounds for no work? That just seems crazy in my mind. Services are being cut left and right, but this council is not interested in the possibility of some free cash, or even the bitcoin themselves. They could convert the majority of the BTC into fiat and save a handful for the future and if the price does rise massively, they could become the wealthiest council in all the land.

- Care must be taken when auto copying and pasting Bitcoin addresses. Hackers have made sneaky programs, known as clippers, that can interfere with the pasting process. To be attacked this way would be very unlikely, however, it is prudent for people to know and understand how to protect themselves. This type of attack is known as 'a man in the middle attack'. Should your PC be infected with the hacker's program, it springs its attack the moment you paste an already copied address into your wallet. You might happily copy your recipients' address, from an email for example, but when you paste it into the *send to* field in your wallet, the hacker's program alters the address to one that they control. You may be unaware that this switch has taken place and happily click the send button. This will send your coins directly to the hacker's wallet. It is always best practice having pasted an address, to double-check the entire address character by character to check it is still correct and has not been altered. Some people will check that only the first and last, 4-8 characters are the same as the one you copied. As it is unlikely that a hacker can randomly generate an address where the first and last few characters are the same as your recipient's address. This is unlikely but *not* impossible. So, to be 100% sure the address has been pasted correctly, and especially if large sums are being transferred, please check the address in its entirety.

- Do not send crypto to anyone who is offering you free crypto in return! If you live by the saying 'there is no such thing as a free lunch' it's unlikely you will get caught out by this scam. People on social media have scammed people into sending them crypto, usually by making a fake account of a crypto celebrity or businessperson. They were stating that if individuals sent them a small amount of crypto (to 'open a channel' so to speak) they would send back much more. Unfortunately, many people are fooled by this simple scam, known as the Advanced Fee Scam.

- Make backups! As you now know when you initialise your Bitcoin wallet for the first time you will be prompted to write down your 12-24 word seed phrase. It would be wise to make a second copy (a backup) of these words (again only on paper) and store them in a safe place, or with a family member you trust. If large amounts of crypto are at stake then maybe a safe deposit box or solicitor/custody agent could be considered. Also, consider what could happen to those words over the intervening months or years. Be that through water damage, ageing of the paper or pen ink etc. Periodically checking these to assess the integrity of the paper and wording would be prudent. (Leaving it 20 years and then seeing the words have faded away, or that the paper has badly deteriorated would be most upsetting). As I stated more than once earlier **do not make digital copies of your seed phrase!** No digital photos, no storing it on your PC or uploading it to somewhere like Dropbox/iCloud. These words should only ever be handwritten and *never* be digitised or touch the internet! For those of you that are extra security-conscious (or paranoid), you may even want to consider covering your computer's webcam when jotting the words down in the first place. After all, you never know who's looking at you through that spy cam, I mean webcam. For people who are storing large sums and/or those who wish to give themselves the best long term protection, I have already mentioned the fix. It is the Capsule from the company Cryptosteel. Their stainless steel backup solution will protect your seed phrase from fire, flood, and other threats for a lifetime.

- Limit who you tell about your crypto investing.
  Unlike regular banking, where your fiat is to some degree protected, you do not want every Tom, Dick and Harry to know what your crypto worth is. There have already been some high-level thefts and home invasions in the space. It is one thing telling your family and close friends if you have a couple of hundred pounds worth of BTC, but care should be taken if you own large amounts of crypto.

- Use an alternate email address when interacting with online cryptocurrency exchanges, and even crypto in general. This is simply good practice, to shield your normal email address from any crypto footprint you may start creating. One website you can use to see if your email address has ever been involved in any data breach is the free site https://haveibeenpwned.com which will quickly show you the results it finds and may help you in deciding whether you should ditch an email address and create a new one.

- Use strong and different passwords! Don't use the same password that you use for Facebook, for example, to also log into your cryptocurrency exchange! Don't be lazy, reduce the chance of yourself being hacked. Best practice is to have different passwords for every site you use. Obviously, you should not use easily knowable/guessable (or easily searchable) information in your passwords such as your name or date of birth, or any special date associated to you or your family. Your child or pet's name would also be considered insecure. Strong passwords should be as long as possible (preferably 12 or more characters) and similar to a crypto address, it should ideally be a string of random-looking characters, including upper and lowercase letters and also numbers. Adding special characters such as @<+*&?! adds an extra level of complexity to your password, which makes it even harder for a would-be attacker. A YouTube channel by Rex Kneisley (aka CryptoDad) has a nice explainer video titled *How to Choose a Strong Password with Entropy*. This will teach you some of the basics and will allow you to make yourself a strong password. There are also software programs called password managers that we can use to generate and store complex passwords for us. Not only that, when we need access to the passwords it is storing, it can also auto-fill them into our websites at the point of logging in. All we need to do is set and remember just one very strong password. That one password is all you will ever need from that point forward, as the password manager will do the rest for you. Three programs that at the time of writing are recommended by many different sources are Dashlane, LastPass and 1Password. Antivirus software such as Norton and McAfee also offer this service within their programs.

- Use two-factor authentication (2FA) on all accounts where possible. 2FA is sometimes referred to as two-step verification. Most of you may be familiar with this already in some way shape or form. Many high street banks in the UK now supply their customers with a device called a PINsentry, which is a little calculator looking device. Having inserted your bank card into the PINsentry and proved your identity by tapping in your card's PIN, the device generates an eight-digit number, known as an OTP (one-time-password). You must then use this number to log into your online bank account or to validate purchases on some websites. The OTP is only valid for a short time before it becomes useless and a newly generated number is needed. Another version of 2FA is when we receive a text or email to validate our login requests for example, which again generally offers us an OTP or makes us follow a specific link. Traditional 2FA security makes us prove that we are the owner of an account by requiring us to know two things (hence the name *two-factor* authentication). This is achieved by proving that we know something, and also that we physically have something, such as 1) Knowing our password 2) Having access to our email account, our bank card, pin or phone (in the case of receiving SMS). Cryptocurrency exchanges and other platforms also use this security feature to add an extra layer of protection to their user's accounts. They may text your phone with a code which is required at the point of logging in for example, known as text-based two-factor authentication.

Although this additional security in the form of a text is sensible, our phones can be susceptible (see SIM swapping below) so using a special 2FA app is preferable.

Google has a 2FA app called Google Authenticator, which you can download to your phone for free. It generates six-digit OTPs every 30 seconds and once linked to your favourite websites, you can use these OTPs to log into them. When you first use the app to link it to a website, such as a crypto exchange, you will be shown a long back-up code from the website provider. I strongly recommend that you make a note of this code. Then, with these codes written down and safely stored you are protected, so that should you lose your phone, you can easily regain access and are not locked out from logging into the websites that you have protected with the app. Another option is to use a standalone and physical 2FA device such as the YubiKey from the company Yubico. This small USB device performs the same job as the Google Authenticator app, however, as it is separate from your mobile phone, it is generally regarded as being a little more secure.

- SIM swapping. This is not common in the UK but is more prevalent in North America due to how their telecommunication companies operate. The large phone companies are not quite geared up for fighting this new attack vector just yet, which is currently used to target individuals in the space who are public and vocal about their crypto wealth, such as prominent business people, YouTube commentators and celebrity crypto traders. The hacker will start by contacting your phone provider and claim to be you. They will convince your phone company to send them a new SIM card (for your phone) as 'you have lost or damaged your phone'. Once they receive your new SIM they can plug it into their phone and start reaping havoc. They may be able to log into your email accounts (using text-based 2FA) and change your passwords, effectively locking you out and massively hindering your ability to gain access to your emails. Then they can focus their attention onto hacking into the crypto exchange accounts that you may have.

One businessman, Michael Terpin, had an unbelievable $23 million stolen from him using this technique. Why did he have so much crypto held on an exchange and not stored on a hardware wallet I hear you fast learners scream?! Yes, you are right in your quick analysis, as you should only hold small amounts of crypto on exchanges and transfer the majority of your crypto to more secure wallets such as PC and hardware wallets. Through some hard investigative work, Terpin successfully sued the individual who stole the funds and in court, the 21-year-old was ordered to pay Terpin over $70 million in losses and damages.

Terpin is also currently suing the mobile phone provider, AT&T for a whopping $220 million.

If you wish to try to protect yourself from this type of attack, the best advice I can give you is to speak to your phone provider and try to get them to attach a PIN or password to your account. This will then be needed if any changes to your account are requested, including the ordering of a new SIM card. Some people have succeeded while others have gone one step further and requested that important changes to their account including SIM card orders, can only be done at your local branch, in person and with ID. This should not concern new users who are just dipping their feet into Bitcoin and will not be a problem for any individual who uses a hardware wallet. After all, Terpin was taking a great risk leaving so many coins and so much value on an exchange. His defence was that lots of these coins were unsupported by most multi-coin crypto wallets at the time, making it far easier for him to leave them on the exchange, than to download a separate PC wallet for each of the many coins he was holding. However, fast forward to the present day, the new Ledger Nano X hardware wallet can hold up to 100 different coins (in varying amounts) at the same time, with support for virtually all the major coins on the market. This one device is all people now need to protect their cryptocurrency.

- Always check that the URL (website address) of the site you believe you are visiting is correct. Malicious websites known as phishing sites are rife in the space. Always check that there is an 's' present after http as shown here https://www (as the 's' denotes you are on a secure site). Also, check that the spelling of the company you are visiting is spelt correctly and is followed by the correct suffix whether that's .co.uk or .com (and also a new and popular suffix within the blockchain space which is .io).

Another thing to note would be the presence of the padlock symbol that is used in web browsers. This is located by the website address field in your browser. Some hackers out there have very crafty ways of tricking you into believing that their fake website is the real site you wish to visit. In this example, the hacker could register the website name www.facelook.com in the hope that you don't notice the 'b' in Facebook has been switched for an 'l' and that in your haste you followed their dodgy link and logged into their site. Once you have logged into their fake site (which will look identical to the real Facebook site) they have caught you and now have your log in details! In this example, maybe hacking your social media accounts wouldn't be a complete disaster. But it could well have been a crypto exchange you had mistakenly visited. Hopefully, this will never happen to you, but should you get tricked this way you would still be protected if you had activated 2FA onto your crypto exchange accounts. It is important to note, that with text-based two-factor authentication, you would still unfortunately be at risk (as a hacker would have access to your phone). To be much more secure you would need to utilise the Google Authenticator app or a YubiKey. Another way to shield yourself from this type of attack would be to not click on links (especially if you do not know the person who sent it to you). This is all worst-case scenario and is not meant to scare people away from Bitcoin. Hopefully, you are never scammed or attacked in any of these ways but being knowledgeable and prepared in advance is preferable than trying to close the barn door once the horse has bolted. Security falls to the individual in the cryptocurrency space so it makes sense to be prepared.

- Many Bitcoin experts will recommend hardware wallets for newcomers. I also agree that they are good products and therefore am happy to recommend them in this book. However, there are a few points that a user needs to be aware of to be as safe as possible. For those who will be buying one, be sure to read Appendix C at the end of this book for a few tips to increase your knowledge and security while using these devices. Nothing in this life is certain (aside from death and taxes) and this saying rings extremely true in the crypto world. Some people go to great lengths to protect their bitcoin but there can always be a new threat around the next corner. Some years ago, a Bitcoin expert detailed the lengths someone would need to go, to be 100% sure that the Bitcoin software and hardware they are using is 100% safe...and it was impossible! Basically, you had to make it all by yourself. It starts by collecting your own sand. Ok, easy so far. Step two went up a gear, as you now need to refine this sand into silicone. From this state, use the silicone to make your very own computer chip (all by yourself with no assistance from anybody). Repeat this process until you have all the inner components of a PC and then build your very own totally secure computer. Then, from scratch, write your own, brand new, programming language. Then using this 100% new and completely safe language, write your very own wallet software and on and on it went... Therefore, most people have no choice and simply have to trust software/hardware producers and listen to and follow the security advice of the professionals within this new economy. So now that you realise and appreciate that the professionals in the space have done the majority of the hard work for you, be sure to check Appendix C if you intend to do the right thing and protect your cryptocurrency with a hardware wallet.

- Earlier we briefly mentioned a function known as multisig. This stands for multiple signatures, and is the security feature which gives multiple people their own private key for the *same* crypto address. A specified ratio of these people is needed to sign a transaction for it to become valid and to be broadcast on the network.

For example, a CEO along with the Chief Financial Officer and the Chief Technology Officer could all have their own private key to the same company wallet. To transfer funds out of the company wallet, two of the three people would need to sign the transaction. You can scale those figures and ratios dependant on your needs, for example, you could set up an 8 of 12 multisig wallet. In this case, at least 8 of the 12 board members must sign, for a transaction to move the bitcoin. It might also become a good way for parents to protect their child's Bitcoin wallet. A 2 of 3 multisig wallet would require that at least one parent along with the child, sign the transaction for it to be processed. Little Timmy can no longer spend his cryptocurrency willy-nilly on chocolate and video games without parental supervision. This system can also be used to allow holders to protect themselves from physical theft. In this example of a robust 3 of 4 multisig, a private key could be given to yourself, your solicitor, best friend and your auntie who lives abroad. Even if an attacker had gained access to your key they would still need access to another two keys for the heist to commence. Most Bitcoin addresses start with the digit 1 however, a multisig address starts with the digit 3.

It is not my intention to scare or worry a newcomer to this space, but I do intend to make you as security conscious as possible. **As you hopefully now understand, security is no joke, as in many cases there is no support number you can call to ask for help. For example, remember there is no renew password button in Bitcoin!** As we learnt early on in this book, Bitcoin is a push network meaning unlike bank and credit card transactions, they cannot be reversed. Yes, there are services and forums and individuals on the internet who can help you, but as Bitcoin is a decentralised monetary system, where the responsibility falls on the end-user…well, the responsibility falls on you. People should take some time to think about how they wish to protect themselves when entering this space and become their own bank. For those looking to jump in with both feet and who know they are planning to make the most of this financial revolution, they should consider some of the following options.

- Consider getting a password manager, to massively reduce the likelihood of your various accounts being hacked into due to using weak and repeated passwords.

- Maybe the more advanced, security or privacy-focused individuals could consider signing up for a VPN service (Virtual Private Network) to help shield their IP address when on the internet.

- Buying a hardware wallet is a fairly good investment in my opinion, especially if you are planning to put a half-decent amount of fiat into cryptocurrency.

- Use 2FA via the Google Authenticator app or YubiKey wherever possible.

- Taking the time to consider how to protect your seed phrase would be time well spent. This could be achieved by using the mother of all backups, the Capsule from Cryptosteel.

- How will you pass this information on to your loved ones, so that should you 'get hit by a bus' the backup is still protected. Do not let your demise also be the end of any crypto inheritance that your family may well be relying on.

If you're only looking to buy a tiny fraction of a bitcoin then maybe you don't need to worry too much. But as your crypto investment grows (either through additional investment or the price rising) so should your measures in protecting it. Security can be a worrying aspect of cryptocurrency, especially as so much of the technology and terminology is currently alien to many of us. Some basic security measures are all that a newcomer to this space needs along with the understanding that they are responsible for their money, and that they should ideally use best practices. The exchanges Kraken and Binance will happily hold your keys/crypto for you until you take the next step and download either a PC wallet or buy yourself a hardware wallet. When you do go solo, and take full control of your crypto, protecting your seed phrase is the most important measure you need to do. Followed by trying your absolute best to use different and strong passwords.

If interacting with online services and exchanges then using 2FA is also a no brainer. Don't become an easy target to the scammers and hackers, make it hard for them and they will quickly move on to the easier targets.

FACEBOOK'S LIBRA

I'm sure many of you reading this book heard the news in the summer of 2019 of Facebook's plan to release their own cryptocurrency. Some of you, however, may not have heard what followed. The news sent a shockwave around the planet and before the dust had settled many countries were voicing their concerns.

Facebook had announced its plan to release a Stablecoin called Libra. Like all Stablecoins, it is designed to be price stable, meaning it would only fluctuate by a cent or two in either direction and would always be worth around $1. It would never rise in value like bitcoin and most other cryptocurrencies. It is also reported that it may have smart contract capabilities like ETH. Libra had been designed to compete with the likes of PayPal and even Western Union to some degree, as it was expected that anyone with a Facebook or WhatsApp account would be able to freely send these 'Libra dollars' to one another in a frictionless and fast manner. Who is backing the project? Instead of running like Bitcoin, where anyone can connect to the network to mine blocks, Libra is run on an invitation-only network. They had been working hard behind the scenes and had created *The Libra Association* that would help manage the network. I won't list all the names but many of the biggest companies in America are members, including Mastercard, Visa, Uber, PayPal, eBay and Spotify, along with some large venture capital companies. Another interesting point is that each company will have to cough up $10 million to be included. On the face of it, Libra sounded like good press for cryptocurrency, especially if you can try to forget for one minute that it is being developed by one of the least privacy focussed companies on the planet. It would have raised awareness massively and highlighted the technology to their user base of 2.6 billion people. In turn, they would have been introduced to Bitcoin and the other leading cryptocurrencies and many would have undoubtedly adopted the fairer and less centralised versions.

Why am I using the words could have and would of? Because many nations around the world had a very negative opinion of Libra the instant it was announced. France, India and Russia instantly stated that Libra would not be allowed to operate within their countries. Well, that's a massive chunk of Zuckerberg's customer base gone before the project has even left the gate. Who was next to voice their opinion? Most countries around the globe had something negative to say, but at the top of the list was the American government. In the following weeks, executives from the company behind Facebook's Libra, a company called Calibra, were invited to a two day hearing with the Senate Banking Committee in America. Here things did not go to plan for Calibra and Facebook. Even before the hearing took place, the US government had sent a letter to Calibra advising them to halt all work on the Libra project. For some reason, the American government were concerned that a private company such as Facebook could release their own crypto asset that can ultimately compete with (and possibly undermine) the US national currency. Their currency, which since 1913 has been used to control much of the world's people. For some reason, they were not very impressed with Zuckerberg's plans of creating his own 'dollar' overnight with a flick of a switch.

To give the senators their credit, they were also quick to highlight their concerns regarding Facebook's track history with regards to security breaches and misuse of user information. Many stating that they could not imagine letting a company with such a bad history, loose with the ability to control a new type of currency and then be able to freely monitor how people are spending these 'Zuck-Bucks'. We are now finally all aware of how Facebook sells user data to the highest bidder from their social media platform, well the senators were wise enough to twig that the same thing would happen with all the data collected from the new Libra network. It was quite interesting hearing senators slam Libra and in the same sentence praise Bitcoin. The executives from Calibra were sent packing with their tails between their legs and told to hold off developing the Libra coin until further notice. It is expected that Facebook and Calibra have done no such thing and are still developing the coin and are striving for a release date sometime in 2021.

The latest motion from within the American government is the plan to release a bill to ban large tech companies making their own cryptocurrencies. It would seem this Libra coin has shaken the US government to its core, and they are wanting to stop a potential tsunami of American companies all wanting to release their own coins. Two months later, PayPal withdrew themselves from the Libra association and it is rumoured that Visa and Mastercard may also withdraw. Many people will watch with interest to see how this story develops, however, it was very refreshing to hear the members of the United States government 'big up' Bitcoin in such a public forum.

GLOBAL ADOPTION AND DEVELOPMENT

It is hard to convey how much development there is in the crypto space. Even if we just focus on Bitcoin, it is nearly impossible to show you how fast-paced the development and adoption is moving. I've heard one person liken it to dog years and it's very true. Closely following the crypto news and its developments is like cramming seven years of regular news and politics into one year, ouch, that would make your head spin. Seven years of politics squeezed into one year, no thanks! Thankfully, Bitcoin is much cooler and fascinating. If you have enjoyed what you have read I hope that you visit some of the news sites I have listed at the end of this book. At least then you will gain some appreciation of the various developments in the space. It's almost as if the news channels could dedicate a slot to their shows to report on some of the more important, groundbreaking and serious crypto news. Below I have included just a few recent stories and developments.

- We now have companies issuing cryptocurrency debit cards, allowing users to spend their crypto in any establishment that accepts Visa and Mastercard. The software 'behind' the card converts your bitcoin instantly into fiat right there at the chip and pin device, allowing you to spend crypto and for the retailer or restaurateur to receive government currency. UK companies offering 'crypto-cards' include Revolut and Wirex. One card that serves the US market is BitPay. This is all achieved instantly with no need to wait for the confirmations usually expected with Bitcoin and other crypto transactions. Many Bitcoin payment solutions now exist for merchants across the world, basically offering the same service as described above. They can accept bitcoin but also request that a percentage of the transaction is instantly converted into their fiat currency (this is all handled by the payment provider).

This allows the merchant to stay in their fiat currency and not have to spend time and money transferring back and forth, but also gives them exposure to bitcoin and is a clever way of slowly accumulating this asset. Merchants around the world who accept bitcoin and other cryptocurrencies, tend to sell their products at a reduced rate if the buyer uses crypto.[28] Aside from the various fees the merchant might be saving, many simply value bitcoin and will happily sell their goods at a discount to acquire these new and rare digital assets.

- The list of prominent businesspeople that applaud Bitcoin is forever growing. The Twitter and Square CEO Jack Dorsey has become a big fan of Bitcoin. His latest company, Square, has released the most popular financial app in America called Cash App, which allows US customers to invest in the traditional market but to also buy and hold bitcoin. The CEO of Tesla and SpaceX, Elon Musk, seems impressed with the technology but has stated he does not own any (aside from the 0.25 BTC a friend gave him). When will Tesla cars have their own inbuilt cryptocurrency wallet? Countless other companies are investing or learning what the benefits of adopting Bitcoin (or blockchain tech) can do for their company and customers. Some big names who *are* currently testing what this new technology can offer are UPS, FedEx, Nike, Unilever, Nestle, United healthcare Group, Allianz and the pharmaceutical giant Roche to name but a few.

---

[28] The business will often make a saving, as they are not being charged by a bank or credit card company. Merchants can also suffer from what is known as a chargeback, where people make a dispute over a particular credit card payment. The card company tend to side with the customer and reverse the payment. Reversing payments cannot happen in Bitcoin, so many merchants will make a saving from that simple fact alone.

- Many countries around the world are constructing legislation to allow their citizens and businesses to use and even earn cryptocurrency. Here in the UK, HMRC recently issued its latest guidelines on how crypto investors, traders and even people who earn crypto need to pay their taxes. The IRS in America also recently updated its guidelines. Ernst & Young, one of the top four auditing and accounting companies, have announced the launch of a new tool to help people with their cryptocurrency tax reporting. Some states in America have passed legislation allowing state taxes to be paid directly in bitcoin and not solely the US dollar. Also, the software company Microsoft have recently included the bitcoin currency symbol into Excel, their well-known spreadsheet software.

- Many universities around the world are now offering blockchain or smart contract courses and degrees. To drop a few names there is Cornel, MIT, New York, Nicosia in Cyprus, Europea in Madrid, University of Edinburgh, the IT University of Copenhagen in Denmark, SP Jain in India and amongst many others the online academy in the UK B9lab.

- Many organisations are spreading the word of crypto throughout Africa, South America, and the developing world, where adoption is growing fast. One system called M-Pesa designed by Vodafone, allows Africans to use their old fashioned Nokia style feature phones to send regular fiat currency to each other via SMS. The crypto company Bitwala is now allowing people to send bitcoin to their M-Pesa account. This integration now allows millions of M-Pesa users to easily send bitcoin with their feature phone across Kenya, Tanzania, Afghanistan, South Africa, Romania, and Albania.

- The United Nations Children's Fund more commonly referred to as UNICEF have started accepting donations in bitcoin and ether. Other charities that accept bitcoin include The Royal National Lifeboat Institution, Save the Children, Watsi, Free Snowden, The American Red Cross, WikiLeaks, Khan Academy and FreeRoss. I imagine that many lesser-known charities are also accepting crypto and that in the future many more will adopt the tech, as they discover the financial benefits of what holding onto these assets for a few months or even years can bring.

- The company Blockstream have hired access to a network of satellites that orbit the planet and have uploaded the Bitcoin blockchain onboard. These five satellites that hang 22,000 miles above us, beam an up-to-date copy of the Bitcoin blockchain to all corners of the planet. Using their signal receiving hardware, their 'Bitcoin Mesh Network' ensures the Bitcoin blockchain is accessible even if the internet is down in any region of the world. This method can also be used to deliver Bitcoin to places without the existing infrastructure for mass adoption. Parts of Africa, the South Americas and Asia may struggle with their limited internet, but this service could enable adoption to grow in these areas. Another separate scientific development includes piggybacking Bitcoin transactions onto radio waves, which could become a handy solution for people and communities with limited resources. While elsewhere, futurist thinkers see a coming age where firing a 'Bitcoin transacting laser' from your off-world colony to a neighbouring planet or orbiting space station, or a passing mining colony on an asteroid a reality, and are now focusing on the science involved.

- While back here on earth, UK football supporters may already be aware that Watford and Southampton football clubs both have the Bitcoin logo on their club's strip.

This is courtesy of a deal with the sports betting and casino company Sportsbet.io. While across the planet many sportsmen and women are starting to ask their clubs, promoters, and sponsors to pay them in bitcoin.

- The company ICE, which owns the New York Stock Exchange has launched a cryptocurrency futures trading platform. They spent a long time trying to seek approval from the American regulators, and in August 2019 it was finally approved, and their platform called Bakkt will allow for more institutional traders to enter the space. It is reported that Bakkt has partnered with the likes of Microsoft and the coffee giant Starbucks. The American asset management company Fidelity is also entering the space. They have trillions of dollars under management, with one of its mutual funds alone managing over $100 billion. It is also the largest American retirement plan provider with a massive $1.4 trillion. Their crypto-specific platform called Fidelity Digital Assets will allow their customers to buy bitcoin. The large Dutch bank ING is also offering their customers Bitcoin wallets, while the Japanese e-commerce giant Rakuten is now offering Bitcoin wallets to their customers along with the ability to trade fiat to crypto. Rakuten, which is likened by some people to the 'Amazon of Japan' also operates Japan's largest online bank, along with having a large share of the Japanese credit card market. With the various companies they control, spread over 29 countries they serve over 1 billion customers. How long until they offer their banking customers a Bitcoin wallet? These last four big companies alone will introduce lots of people and legitimacy to Bitcoin and cryptocurrency.

- The Samsung S10 smartphone has a Blockchain Keystore built into the phone, (meaning it can store private keys on the device) turning the S10 into a hardware wallet. It is reported to currently support 33 different cryptocurrencies including bitcoin, ether, the Stablecoin TrueUSD and the Binance exchange token BNB. Will the next iPhone follow suit? Samsung has also announced that they plan to release their own crypto token and have also made a large investment with the hardware wallet company Ledger. Are they looking to integrate their token and hardware wallet capabilities into their future phones and smart TVs?

- In late 2019 Brian Armstrong, the CEO of the cryptocurrency exchange Coinbase, tweeted the following. "Whether institutions were going to adopt crypto or not was an open question 12 months ago. I think it's safe to say we now know the answer. We're seeing $200-$400 million a week in crypto deposits come in from institutional investors". It has also been reported that they are now holding $7 billion in deposits for all their customers, with $1 billion being held specifically for the institutional investors they serve.

- A recent poll completed by hundreds of the world's top executives showed that 70% believe they need to adopt blockchain technology or risk being left behind. As an example of this, there is a large alliance of car manufacturers that have teamed together to form the *Mobility Open Blockchain Initiative* (Mobi). A few big names from this organisation are IBM, BMW, Ford, Honda, Renault and GM.

- Microsoft has announced they are about to develop an identity management solution on the Bitcoin blockchain, while Google and Amazon have recently released services that allow customers to produce their own blockchains at a click of a button. Many smaller companies have already been offering this service for several years now, but with these global heavyweights now entering the space the future looks bright for Bitcoin and blockchain technology.

- Recent legislation in America is allowing banks to enter the crypto space, and PayPal were quick to jump in. Banks in the US can now offer custody services for their customers. This will also bring lots of attention to this new economy. I imagine it will only be a matter of time before other countries follow suit.

- Many large companies are starting to buy bitcoin. For one example we have the now legendary proponent of bitcoin, Michael Saylor, who just converted the majority of his company's treasury money from in his words, the failing US dollar, into the world's hardest money - bitcoin! This was to the tune of an unbelievable $425 million!

- The Oxford English Dictionary has included the word Satoshi in their most recent edition. This is in reference to the smallest unit within a bitcoin and shows me that slowly, this new technology is knitting itself into the fabric of our society.

These have just been a few headlines to pass my desk. There are literally dozens if not hundreds more that could have made this section. I find it very strange that the mainstream media do not report any of these worthy stories. As I'm sure you must now appreciate Bitcoin is big. It is not just a new type of money with a few hundred hours of development behind it. It is a new economy and a massive industry, with hundreds of thousands of hours of research, scientific and business development behind it. One that has the might and determination to advance global chip manufacturing and also to piggyback the blockchain onto a network of satellites.

WAYS TO ACQUIRE BITCOIN

If you are interested in taking advantage of this new technology, here are the four ways you can acquire your first bitcoin.

<u>Mining</u>. As we have learnt you can mine bitcoin, but this is not necessarily advisable for beginners. Maybe mining the smaller, GPU friendly coins would be more suitable as you can then trade these cheaper coins for bitcoin.

<u>You can earn bitcoin</u>. If your employer/customer is open to the suggestion you could ask that all, or a percentage of your salary/invoice is paid to you in bitcoin. Remember you will still need to pay your income tax and any capital gains taxes.

<u>Gifts/Tips</u>. Some people are tipped bitcoin and other cryptos for helping individuals on forums for offering helpful advice, or for offering other services. The French street artist Pascal Boyart, for example, added a Bitcoin QR Code to his artwork which he painted onto a wall and has already received over one bitcoin to his address. I'm sure as time goes on tipping in crypto will become much more common, with waiters and waitresses possibly having their own QR Codes readily available for people to tip them with.

<u>Buy bitcoin</u>. For those of you already certain that you are going to buy some bitcoin, head over to my website <u>https://www.thebitcoinbook.co.uk</u> and follow the link to join the exchange Kraken. Remember that in Appendix B of this book I include a helpful guide to show you how to use Kraken to get your first bitcoin.

WHAT KIND OF BITCOINER WILL YOU BECOME?

Once you have decided that you want to buy some bitcoin and have settled on how you are going to acquire it, you may find that over time your opinion changes, as to what 'type' of Bitcoiner you are. One example of this is you may have originally entered the space solely for the financial gains that you have heard others have experience. Then over time, you may have developed a keen interest in the ethics or economics of Bitcoin, and now the financial gains are secondary to the freedom or anti-inflationary features of the technology.

As your interests or beliefs change, you may also find that your opinions or alignments with companies in the space also change. For example, after getting your first bitcoin you may see people on the internet bashing your favourite exchange, or they may sneer at the way you hold your coins. As unlike them, you may use a third party custodian wallet to hold your coins. Or if you do use a PC or hardware wallet, you don't use the particular one they use. Firstly, let us establish the facts. You are your own boss, and you are the person who decides where and how you spend or save, along with who you decide to do business with. These are your decisions and yours alone. Once you have been in the space for a while and have learnt a little more, there is no harm in you branching out from your beginning position and strengthening your security or moving up the ladder of custody and taking control of your own keys. Earlier we learnt the meme, 'not your keys not your bitcoin' and how this was born out of a desire to control your own keys and not let a third party do it for you. Securing your keys yourself is seen as being a giant step for a newcomer, and if acquiring the bitcoin in the first place is the first hurdle to jump, storing your own keys is the second hurdle. The third hurdle, and the one that most people in the space are still far from completing, is to run their own node.

This brings us to the next meme, 'don't trust, verify'. This is where individuals should aspire (in some people's minds) to operate their own node. Having your own node means you will be able to:

- Help to service and uphold the infrastructure of the Bitcoin network.

- Verify your own transactions personally. As opposed to trusting another node operator that the coins/transactions you received are legitimate.

This third hurdle is the pinnacle of a true Bitcoiner (whatever that is) and for this reason, many people have yet been able to clear it. For this reason, you will find 99% of all Bitcoiners somewhere between having landed from jumping the first hurdle to gearing themselves up to attempt the third.
Do not think you need to buy additional equipment and start running a node on day one. Just focus on entering the new economy if that is your desire and aim to be as safe as possible. There is plenty of time for you to learn more and increase your personal involvement in the network.

Companies are now selling ready to go nodes, fresh from a box, plug and play. But currently, it is something that only the diehards undertake along with whales, entrepreneurs, businesses, and the serious hobbyists. If you are computer-savvy you can make your own node for a couple of hundred pounds. Whether you make your own or buy an off the shelf unit, once you have your own node you can (all by yourself) verify all the transactions you (and everyone else) makes and receives. You no longer need to rely on the larger companies in the space or even the hardware wallet providers. It is important to note that once the bitcoin is in your wallet and a few confirmations have passed, you can rest assured that you own the bitcoin. In using a hardware wallet, you interface with the manufacturer's software and node, so in doing so you 'share' very small pieces of data about your transactions.

Most people do not believe this is a massive issue, as it is only a small amount of data and the wallet operators are responsible with what they do gather, but this small 'leak of data' is one that cypherpunks and other privacy-focused individuals in the space would rather not tolerate. They are here to take *complete* ownership of their financials and in doing so hold their *own* keys and verify their *own* transactions. Most Bitcoiners don't use their own node, so you should not be put off by the last few sentences. I have only included this information so you are fully aware of the heights you can aim for in the quest for being fully sovereign with your own wealth. I believe in the future, running your own node will become a lot more widespread than it is today, along with the use of the Lightning Network and other technologies that will 'sit on top' of the Bitcoin base protocol. If Bitcoin is still here in 5-10 years, you may well see many homes utilising their own node. Today it seems strange to enter a house that doesn't have a microwave or a TV, well in the future a family home that does not have its own crypto node could be strange.

I have only recommended services and products in this book (Kraken, Binance, Ledger and Cryptosteel) to friends, family, and my readers that I feel provide a brilliant user experience coupled with top-class security. Only time will tell what kind of Bitcoiner you become, but regardless of the companies you interact with I hope you stay safe and secure.

BITCOIN INVESTING/TRADING

I Bought a quarter of a bitcoin when I first heard of it and sold most of it near the top of the 2017 price rise. The profit paid for the removal costs in moving to a new house, along with some of our living expenses while I was off work recovering from my operation. My financial flutter with bitcoin was short-lived and although it worked in my favour, the reader should be wary as nothing is certain. Remember my disclaimer from the beginning of this book and please strive to learn as much as possible about investing and trading in cryptocurrency before you start. Also, you should follow these two simple rules.

- Never borrow fiat to invest or trade cryptocurrency.

- Never invest or trade with fiat that you cannot afford to lose.

Hopefully, these are self-explanatory. If the crypto market moves against you, you can quickly end up losing your capital. In these two examples, you will be putting yourself under unnecessary stress as with the first rule, you will still need to pay the debt back to your lender regardless of the outcome. With regards to the second rule, you could be making life difficult for yourself, if you lose money that you cannot afford to lose. It will have a detrimental effect on your standard of living and you may be unable to pay for upcoming bills or worst case, food for yourself or your family.

A third rule (which does not relate to investing per se but to trading) is to not trade using leverage, which is also known as margin. Unfortunately, many people are unaware of the risks involved when trading, as over 90% of new traders lose their trades *and* capital. (Regular trading without leverage is referred to as *spot trading*). In my opinion, people should steer clear of leveraged trading completely and stick with traditional spot trading if they wish to actively trade. Even saying this, spot trading is also very difficult to be profitable at. Most people in the Bitcoin space just buy and hold. They become a hodler (see Appendix A). Many look to buy and hold for a few years to even a decade or more.

Leveraged trading is where the size of your position is artificially increased beyond the figure you started with.[29] Whereas traditional spot trading is done with 100% of your own capital.

As we know many people have become very wealthy from their early bitcoin investments. There are now even several bitcoin billionaires out there (see the Winklevoss twins for one example). The important piece of information to note here is that many of these individuals bought bitcoin when they were still only pennies or in single or the low double digits. Trying to mimic the gains experienced by these early investors, is going to be extremely risky for most people. Therefore, many newcomers turn to some of the smaller capped coins believing that they can play the same game with these coins that the early bitcoin investors did, and that their chance of becoming a millionaire is restored. Again, take caution as many of these lower-priced coins may not perform as bitcoin has and many of them could quite simply fade away.

---

[29] For example, with 2 times (2x) leverage, you could place a trade with £50 worth of bitcoin, but the exchange will open your trade for you with £100. This means if the trade moves in your favour you can look to gain a lot more, in this example, twice as much. Traders can be enticed into opening trades with much higher leverage, such as 10x, 50x or even up to 125x that some exchanges offer. The big problem with leveraged trading is that if the price moves against you only a tiny fraction, because of the leverage you have set, you are wiped out of your position far sooner than you would have been if you opened the trade with no leverage whatsoever, known as spot trading.

Maybe their developers conducted an ICO and for this reason, the community do not value it highly. Maybe they pre-mined all their coins, which as we learnt earlier (in many people's minds) lessens the perceived value of the coin. Maybe when they pre-mined all the coins, they made many billions, meaning they are not as scarce as you might think, and for that reason alone they may always stay relatively cheap in price. Maybe the developers/business have held onto tens of millions of these coins and are waiting to dump them onto the market for a quick profit when they see fit. All these factors, including many others, can help to establish if a coin will gain any value over its lifetime. Always remember that Bitcoin is special for many of the ways it fairly and organically grew in those early years.

One facet of bitcoin that could have been mentioned anywhere within this book but seems logical to place here, is the price volatility. Volatility is the overall range, or difference, seen in the price swings. Take one look at a bitcoin price chart and you will see that the price moves up and down (sometimes drastically) every day and on the longer term it also swings massively month to month and year on year. All markets are volatile. Houses, stocks, and gold all experience this economic feature to some degree, but bitcoin is extremely young in comparison and is currently very prone to it. This can be a worrying prospect for a newcomer especially as we have grown accustomed to our fiat currency being much more price stable. Although, as you may now be discovering through having read this book, our government currency is not very price stable. It loses its value, albeit slowly over time. I think at this point, readers and adopters of this technology need to realise that bitcoin is not quite an out-and-out digital cash just yet (although it obviously can be used as a currency). It is slowly maturing, but because its price has increased over the years many people are holding on to it rather than spending it. Over time, as the price flattens, or as people are happy with the rise they have experienced, they will be happy to spend their coins. Volatility is another factor, and we may see it become used more like digital cash in the future once its volatility stabilises, but for now, bitcoin is more akin to a commodity and behaves more like gold.

Volatility is natural when a market or ecosystem is small. Experts know that this volatility will smooth out as this new digital economy increases in size. Its volatility has already decreased since it was first invented. In the coming future when Bitcoin's adoption is dozens of times greater than it is today, the volatility or the percentage swings seen in any given hour, day, week, or month will be much smaller. As it stands now, many day traders and speculators quite enjoy this function.

To a beginner, it is concerning but to a trader or financially savvy individual, these swings are heavenly. These high and low swings make this new digital economy appear like the Wild West to a trained person and is one reason why so many investors and traders are running towards bitcoin with open arms.

Having said all of this, if we take a step back from the chart and look at the bigger picture (the long term trend) we can see bitcoin has always performed outstandingly. As we learnt earlier, it has (possibly) experienced a 9,000,000% return in the last decade alone. It has been the best performing financial asset ever! The volatility is high, but over the long term, the price has always gone up. We can see every four years or so there is a massive correction, or crash, or popping of the bubble but again this is normal for *all* markets and commodities. This four-year time frame is interestingly similar to many other markets and is also strengthened due to the four-year halving of the block reward we discussed earlier. Either way, every time there has been a large correction in the price, it has eventually stabilised and then pushed back up higher than the previous high. For example, in early 2011 its price hit parity with the US dollar and a few months later it reached £25 and then crashed back down. By 2013 it had recovered and a new high of over £800 was reached. Again, the price slumped, but four years later in 2017 it climbed to £15,000.

These boom and bust cycles are normal and will be expected for many years to come until the volatility smooths.

Anyone interested in investing their fiat into bitcoin would be well advised to do lots of homework on the subject. I will list a few resources and names I have heard over the last few years for those readers who wish to enter this new economy solely for the financial speculation. One concept of investing a person may want to learn is called dollar-cost averaging. This is a method many people use to invest in cryptocurrency and other financial markets. Instead of dropping all their capital in at once, they scale into a position every week or month regardless of the price. Some people believe that the 'all in at once' approach is more successful while others feel that slowly and consistently entering the market will, over time, even out any of the rises and drops in the price and smooths out your cost of entry. Another aspect of trading and investing is Technical Analysis. This skill may be useful to anyone who wishes to learn how to trade and is briefly explained in Appendix B. Below is a small list of names who will be able to teach you some of the fundamentals of investing and trading bitcoin. A simple internet or YouTube search and you will uncover lots of valuable information from these people.

- Willy Woo - A Bitcoin famous analyst, investor and entrepreneur.

- Alessio Rastani - A traditional trader turned whistle-blower and now a crypto analyst and trader who has his own YouTube channel.

- Stephan Livera - A podcast host who interviews many prominent individuals. On his channel, you can find an interesting interview, SLP67 with a gentleman known in the space as PlanB. He re-interviews PlanB on the show SLP86 and again on SLP122. These should be listened to in order. In these interviews, PlanB details some of his controversial research into the future bitcoin price, by showing some of the techniques and computer models that he uses from his profession as a money manager for a large hedge fund, which factors in the stock-to-flow ratio we looked at earlier in this book. Another interesting investment-related interview from this podcast series is SLP109 with Preston Pysh.

- Bob Loukas -This trader has an interesting channel on YouTube, where he shows his methods for investing in the space, believing a four-year cycle is present and that with a little skill (luck and good timing) people can take advantage of this new technology and create generational wealth for themselves and their family.

GLOBAL EMERGENCIES

How does Bitcoin fair in an economic downturn? Is it a safe haven asset like gold, that can be relied on more than traditional currencies during recessions or depressions?

Right now, the answers to these questions are unknown. In the coming months and years, we shall see how useful Bitcoin is during periods of uncertainty. Bitcoin was created at the start of the Great Recession. At that time, it was not widely adopted and was unable to help citizens who could have utilised a fair and trusted monetary system. However, now Bitcoin *is* more ingrained within our society and more and more people are learning of it weekly, with many of these people downloading a wallet and buying some bitcoin. As many people see their savings, pensions and purchasing power evaporate, and the likelihood of the world's governments dipping their hands into people's personal bank accounts increase (to bail out their crony friends), many people may look to protect themselves by turning to the world's first open and fair cryptocurrency.

As this book goes to print, we are currently experiencing the coronavirus pandemic and simultaneously sitting on the brink of another major economic meltdown. How Bitcoin will react to these and other global emergencies is unclear at this time. In March 2020, we saw the S&P 500 stock index drop over 30% in value (it was the largest drop in such a short time in recorded history) and bitcoin followed and even dropped more. Implying that Bitcoin *is* correlated (linked) with the traditional markets. However, many pundits and analyst believe that Bitcoin is uncorrelated with the traditional system and therefore could help people in times of need. The global market has momentarily started to recover from the initial slump, whereas bitcoin has already totally recovered and is now higher than it was before the March crash!

Some people believe the recent drop in bitcoin's price is due to how easy it is to cash out of bitcoin compared to other financial markets and products in times like this. Many people the world over are trying to get back into cash quickly as the liquidity crisis worsens, however, many will be facing delays and push back from their broker or asset manager. Many professionals know that it only takes a percentage of people to move assets and currency for the house of cards to collapse. Or for bank runs to start as we all saw in 2008, with people desperately queuing to get their money out of the failing banks. Bitcoin, however, has allowed many to cash out of their positions easily and is one reason why the bitcoin price dropped as it did. It has since recovered though, and as the price of gold climbed in 2008 bitcoin seems set to follow on a similar path.

It now looks like *The Everything Bubble* I spoke of at the start of this book is likely to collapse in on itself. This current hundred-year experiment with fiat currency could be coming to an end with the central banks of this world now racing to attain 0% (or even negative) interest rates, the lowest in thousands of years. We are starting to see an intensification of quantitative easing, with billions more pounds and dollars being pumped into the system weekly to try and prop everything up. Reports in England of the worst economic slump for 300 years have also been made! All this financial turmoil only goes to highlight how poorly conceived and managed our financial system is. The abandonment of hard money a hundred years ago has destroyed many people's lives over the intervening decades. The destruction of the nuclear family is just one casualty, thanks to the ill-thought-out, Keynesian and government policies. Once upon a time, a family could happily thrive and support itself with just one breadwinner. Now both parents need to work, and sadly in many cases, one or even both must work more than one job. The middle class is slowly being systematically destroyed throughout the Western world. All because our policymakers rejected hard money.

Slowly people are waking up to many of the injustices in our modern world. For many people, the wounds of 2008 are still raw. Unfortunately, many of these wounds will be ripped open again. With regards to the pandemic, many people are realising (50 years after the fact) that the slow march towards globalism (which increased its pace in the last decade or two) has left England and America along with most of the West, in a sorry state. In the UK we don't even make our own paracetamol! We have to rely on other nations, with most of our industry being shipped out to China. The true history of this would shock you, as it was planned and signed off by politicians now long retired or dead. Why would wealthy countries like England, America and much of Europe sign up to a system like that? One that on face value only seemed to weaken them.

Was it solely to save money or is there a more nefarious reason, such as to bring the West down a peg or two and give the emerging markets and the Far East, their chance in the sun? More conspiracies I guess, and I shall remove my tin foil fedora one last time. If nothing else, hopefully, next time a pandemic like this sweeps the planet, our nations (courtesy of our politicians) will be more prepared and quicker to react.

History will rightly praise our healthcare providers; however, I hope that the citizens remember how the majority of our politicians and government policies failed us during the health scare and the ensuing financial crisis. How Bitcoin performs in the wake of this crisis and how it helps to protect people during the likely depression, will be if nothing else, interesting to watch.

CLOSING THOUGHTS

Thank you for reading this book! I hope that you have found it interesting and have learnt a lot from it. You now know more about Bitcoin and cryptocurrency than roughly 99.95% of the world's population and have well and truly earnt your Bitcoin Black Belt. For those of you hungry for more information and wish to progress to some of the Dan grades, I have included some further educational resources at the end of this book. Those who are wanting to run even further down the rabbit hole and are aiming for Master status, the internet is all you need to seek your answers. I have been as thorough as I can be while writing this book for newcomers. I hope that some of the technical and security aspects have not put you off crypto. Modern wallets are quite user-friendly and so long as some basic security measures are taken you should have no problems. Testing yourself with small transactions while getting accustomed to Bitcoin and your wallet is a good idea until you have gained just a little experience. Remember to make a paper backup of any recovery seed phrase your wallet issues you with and you should do just fine.

Bitcoin is many things. It is obviously financial, yet it is also political, technical, social, emotional, fantastical, tribal, and philosophical. There are many reasons why a person may want to buy some bitcoin but currently here in the West, many people do not yet see the need for it. As an Orwellian future slowly marches towards us, we may find that Bitcoin or a system very much like it becomes a plusgood way of protecting ourselves. Other reasons why people may want to buy bitcoin include having an interest in the technology and wanting to play around and test it. Or they may wish to move away from the traditional monetary system and aim to preserve their wealth before their government destroys all their purchasing power with their excessive currency printing.

They may have family living in a different country to themselves that they support financially, and are tired of remittance companies taking too much in transaction fees. They may be a company, organisation, government and wish to avoid sanctions imposed on them by the US government, or the UN or any other country or organisation for that matter. (This was the case with WikiLeaks who adopted bitcoin once the US government ordered Visa, Mastercard and PayPal to stop processing all donations). They may be an individual that lives in a country that has capital controls enforced on them such as the people of China, Brazil, Indonesia, Taiwan, Argentina, and Russia along with many more. Or they may live in a country with failing banking systems that are experiencing hyperinflation. They may be a merchant and rather like the idea of selling their goods for cryptocurrency. Another reason may be because they believe it will make them rich. Be wary of this last reason, as buying, trading, and investing in cryptocurrency can be risky. Yes, the potential returns are high but so are the risks. Bitcoin and other cryptocurrencies are very new, and nobody knows how the technology will evolve. Do not invest more than you can afford to lose and do not borrow to buy cryptocurrency. Learn the basics of trading should you want to start and please stay away from leveraged trading, as this should only be done by experienced traders.

There are many aspects of Bitcoin and cryptocurrency that I have not mentioned within this book, either because I didn't want to confuse the reader or because I was unsure if it was necessary at this stage in your learning. My personal journey is far from complete. I'm still learning as I go and to be honest, I have no idea what Taproots are, along with Splicing, Schnorr signatures and Submarine Swaps. Let alone trying to grasp what Merkelized Abstract Syntax Trees are! Yes, these are all real things. New technical aspects of cryptocurrency that could well be normal in a matter of months or years, but at the moment are advanced learning for any wannabe cypherpunk.

My goal has been to introduce Bitcoin to you and give you a well-rounded understanding, to enable you to enter the space safely. Just because you have evolved from a no Coiner to a potential Bitcoiner, do not assume you know it all. For those interested, there is much more to uncover. Like any humble Black Belt should know, your real education starts now! Remember that Appendix A details some of the terminology used within the crypto space. Appendix B gives you tips on how to sign up with Kraken and Appendix C lists some hardware wallet security considerations.

I did have a fourth Appendix, however courtesy to a nameless individual and due to a copyright infringement, I had to remove the Bitcoin white paper from this publication. Please search the internet if you wish to read it. The Bitcoin white paper was written by Satoshi and accompanied the release of Bitcoin on day one. It is the scientific blueprint on how Bitcoin works. It is the document that every developer or computer-savvy individual reads to gain an understanding of how Bitcoin works 'under the bonnet' and to learn what makes it so different from anything that has existed before, and why in the future, cryptocurrency and blockchain technology, may well be counted as two of humanities greatest inventions. Thank you, Satoshi.

At the start of this book, I asked you to wonder how much purchasing power our fiat currency has lost over the last one hundred years. For those of you who didn't look that figure up, sit down and brace yourself. According to www.cobdencentre.org since 1913 when the Federal Reserve of America was first established, the US dollar and British pound have both lost over 90% of their purchasing power. That's how bad the situation is, with trillions of debt dollars and pounds building up and no sensible plan on how to reset the system. The only thing the policymakers know to do is print more money, which is only perpetuating the problem. When a reset finally comes either by our own hand or one that is forced upon us, it will most likely be a very hard pill to swallow.

Maybe a sound and hard money like gold, or a newer digital version, like bitcoin, can help alleviate the problem and act as the parachute that may be needed. There are 180 national fiat currencies around the planet, all operating similarly. If humanity is going to evolve beyond cotton or polyurethane banknotes and copper-nickel coins and reach for the stars, a fast, secure, non-governmental money might be the only way to go. Start fuelling the booster rockets!

I will leave you with one last interesting fact, one that will put bitcoin's limited supply into perspective and seal the deal in highlighting how scarce this digital asset truly is. If all 21 million bitcoin were mined and *evenly* divided up between everyone on the planet, then each person would have roughly 0.00270000 bitcoin (2.7 milli-bits or 270,000 sats). That's quite a small amount of bitcoin, and at today's prices is only around £30. To divide all the coins in such a convenient and fair way would obviously be impossible now, as many people already own dozens or more.

I try my best to show friends and family that fact, and tell them if they wanted to buy *more* than their fair share, they could buy £50, £100 or even a couple of hundred pounds worth today and maybe, just maybe, that will grow into a nice little addition to their pension pot in the next couple of decades. At the time of completing this book, many people believe the price has bottomed out and we are now in another bull market where the price is expected to climb to new all-time highs. We may never see bitcoin's price below £10,000 ever again.

The rocket ship is fully fuelled now and the countdown to take off is about to begin. If you have enjoyed this book there are several ways you can show your appreciation. Please consider recommending it to family, friends, and colleagues.

You could also be so kind as to leave a good review which helps other in their decision making, and remember you can always support me by following the links at my website if you so choose. I look forward to seeing you in the new economy.

This book was illustrated by The Black Shuck.
Liked his work and want to show it? Chuck him a bone using his Bitcoin address.

36ECmuuSeEAU3kFtg6JbiFRfVDUwGBDUwF

FURTHER EDUCATION

— ◆ ◇ ◆ —

There are countless ways that you can further your knowledge about cryptocurrency. Should you prefer reading, watching or listening, I have included a few good resources below that will keep most people occupied for a long time. Many people in the space can teach us a great deal. They may have a YouTube channel, podcast, website, or have written books. One person I shall give credit to is Andreas M. Antonopoulos. His lectures and videos are very thought-inspiring, and he has done a wonderful job in educating tens of thousands of people.[30] He has dozens of videos on YouTube from the many lectures and interviews he has given around the world on the topic of Bitcoin, cryptocurrency and what decentralised ledger technology can offer. Should you not want to utilise any of the information below and would rather do your own investigating, I can include a small list of names that will light the way for your learning and they would be: Andreas from above, Stephan Livera, Peter McCormack, Saifedean Amous, Trace Mayer, Turr Deemeeter, PlanB, Erik Voorhees and Jameson Lopp.

---

[30] Amongst the many other things he has accomplished, he is a co-host of the *Let's Talk Bitcoin* podcast. His technically focused book on Bitcoin titled *Mastering Bitcoin* along with his new book called *Mastering Lightning* are must-reads for anyone looking to learn more on the technical nature of both Bitcoin and The Lightning Network.

Podcasts

UKBitcoinMaster - A deeply passionate British host, with a 'strong bitcoin hand' who covers many news topics and endeavours to help newcomers with his twice weekly show which is also available on YouTube.

Crypto 101 - A good podcast for beginners to the space, especially if listened to from the beginning.

Let's Talk Bitcoin - The longest running podcast on the topic, with well over 400 episodes and co-hosted by Andreas M. Antonopoulos. The network has several different shows within their feed and between them all, there are over 2,500 episodes covering many of the different aspects of cryptocurrency.

What Bitcoin Did - Another British podcast hosted by Peter McCormack who interviews many prominent individuals. If you visit his website/YouTube channel you will find his beginner's guide, titled *The Beginner's Guide to Bitcoin*. This is a 17 part series of interviews with many prominent and knowledgeable individuals, covering many different subjects of Bitcoin.

The Stephan Livera Podcast - Stephan interviews many well-known people in the space. As mentioned earlier the three PlanB interviews are definitely worth a listen, along with the few that focus on hardware wallets (see Appendix C). His shows are also available on YouTube.

Tales from the Crypt - This podcast is suitable for people who seek a more technical understanding of Bitcoin as the hosts often review new software and hardware updates along with interviewing many developers and high-level users.

Film

Banking on Bitcoin - A documentary on Bitcoin which is available on Netflix and YouTube.

UKBitcoinMaster/What Bitcoin Did/Stephan Livera - All these informative shows are available on YouTube.

aantonup - Andreas M. Antonopoulos' YouTube channel.

Websites

The Bitcoin Book - The official online home of this book. I appreciate your support in helping me spread the word and benefits of bitcoin to as many people as possible. Visit my website https://www.thebitcoinbook.co.uk to join Kraken, Binance, purchase the Ledger Nano X hardware wallet and the Capsule.

Btc Privacy.org - This website shows users some handy ways to protect themselves when using bitcoin, especially if they wish to keep their crypto footprint small.

Lopp.net - Another well-known security focussed site, courtesy of Jameson Lopp.

Nakamoto Institute - A popular site for information on Bitcoin.

Coin Desk - A news orientated website.

Cointelegraph - Another popular news website.

Coin Market Cap - The site that lists all available cryptocurrencies and orders them by their total worth, their market cap.

Where to spend bitcoin - A UK website that lists many of the places where you can spend bitcoin. It also has a map of all the Bitcoin ATMs.

Bit Listen - A unique website that shows every bitcoin transaction in real-time. Each transaction is shown as a bubble floating up along the screen. With your speakers turned on you can hear the transactions, as different amounts of BTC have different tones. It's a little bit like watching a musical crypto lava lamp.

Coin 360 - An infographic website which shows striking data on the market size of the various coins.

Coin Market Cal - An economic calendar for the cryptocurrency market.

Crypto Market 360 - An information and research-based website, with a useful beginner's section with many coins explained in articles of only 360 words.

DApp Radar - A website detailing all the decentralised applications in the space.

MyCryptoPedia - Another good website for learning about crypto and blockchains.

Demonocracy - Illustrations showing global debt shown next to known gold and silver reserves.

US Debt Clock - A site showing the shameful debt of all the top nations growing in real-time. Here you can see about eight thousand pounds being added to the UK national debt every second. America is a lot worse with tens of thousands being added every second.

Easy Crypto Hunter - The site that offers off the shelf cryptocurrency mining rigs.

Books

<u>The Bitcoin Book</u> - Hopefully you will recommend this book to colleagues, friends and family members who you feel would be interested in what it offers.

<u>Mastering Bitcoin</u> - The very technically focused book written by Andreas M. Antonopoulos available in paperback, but if you search you can find it for free on the internet.

<u>Mastering Lightning</u> - Another book by Andreas.

<u>The Bitcoin Standard</u> - The book on the history of money, the Gold Standard and what hard money like bitcoin could do for the world. Written by the economist Saifedean Ammous.

<u>The Crypto Factor</u> - A book by Paul Democritou. He has interviewed prominent people in the space and shows how people can succeed in the blockchain generation. It has been compared to some degree to be a modern version of *Think and Grow Rich*.

<u>Think and Grow Rich</u> - Not a crypto book, as it was written 70 years before Bitcoin was invented. First published in 1937 by Napoleon Hill with over 100 million copies sold. It is quite an inspiring read and suitable for anyone interested in personal and financial development.

<u>The Richest Man in Babylon</u> - Another non-crypto book, but very good for anyone wanting to get their 'financial house' in order, written by George Clason. If only I was given a copy of this book to read as a child or even a young adult, as it teaches some important lessons on how to save.

<u>When Money Dies</u> - The book by Adam Fergusson, which details the downward spiral and death of the Weimar Republic and German mark in the early 1920s, following the massive

devaluation of their currency and the subsequent hyperinflation.[31]

The Creature from Jekyll Island - The book by G. Edward Griffin that details the supposed conspiracy on how the American Federal Reserve was created in secret and how it is privately owned.

---

[31] The front cover shows a photo of a person sweeping the road clear of hundreds of banknotes. Not scooping them up to keep, this valueless money was more likely being swept aside so that water could run more freely off the street and down into the drainage system. *If* it were being collected, it would be to burn to cook with or to keep warm.

APPENDIX A
LINGO, SLANG AND ACRONYMS

Bitcoin address: The 'account number' associated with your Bitcoin wallet. The address is actually a location on the blockchain. This number is far longer than a regular bank account number and includes letters and numbers. Just think that you need an email address to receive email, and now in the crypto age, you need a Bitcoin address to receive bitcoin. A Bitcoin wallet can hold many Bitcoin addresses at the same time. A good practice is to use a brand new Bitcoin address for every transaction you wish to receive.

Wallets: A Bitcoin wallet is the place where we store our bitcoin and other cryptocurrencies. We can visualise them as looking similar in some ways to our regular banking apps or PayPal account. They are computer programs that we can download to our PCs and phones. They act as an interface with the Bitcoin blockchain, allowing us to easily see our addresses and the bitcoin or fractions of bitcoin stored there. From our wallet, we can send and receive bitcoin along with view our transaction history.

Blockchain: The Bitcoin blockchain stores all of the transactions as well as all of the Bitcoin addresses and bitcoin within the addresses. It is a bit like a large spreadsheet or digital account book/ledger. It is publicly viewable and tamper-proof. Once information is stored in the blockchain it is irremovable, making Bitcoin censorship-resistant. Transactions are grouped together into small chunks of data, called blocks.

Once a block is processed, it is attached to the blockchain using cryptography and creates a large and strong history of all transactions. Because we can all view the blockchain, we can verify transactions ourselves meaning blockchain/ledger technology removes the need for trusted middlemen like banks. Blockchains are a new technology but many people are now testing their capabilities and seeing how they can store other types of important and sensitive data for us, such as medical records and house ownership deeds, patents, music artist's rights and more.

Node: A computer or server attached to the Bitcoin network which runs the Bitcoin software. These machines which synchronise with one another, store the Bitcoin blockchain and pass transactions from users to the Bitcoin miners. Your average user of Bitcoin does not run a node at the moment, these are operated by hobbyists, privacy-focused individuals and some of the entrepreneurs and companies in the space.

Miner: A miner uses expensive computer hardware to process the transactions. Miners compete with one another to win the Bitcoin block reward. If their computer wins the complex computational task involved during mining, they receive 6.25 bitcoin and add the current block of transactions, to the previous block which in turn creates the blockchain.

Hash: A hash is a computer function that is used in many areas of technology to help us secure data. For example, the passwords we create when joining online companies are hashed before they are stored. It is a way of turning a big piece of data (or large string of characters) into a much smaller set of characters. Cryptography is used to alter the information, so that what you are left with, no longer resembles the original data, or input as it is called. In Bitcoin, the transactional information, such as addresses involved in the transaction, the amount of bitcoin being sent and a timestamp are hashed together to create one single number, called a hash value.

This is what gets stored on the blockchain, we can almost think of it as a cryptographic receipt.

Block reward: The number of new coins that are issued into circulation every time a new block is added to the blockchain by a miner. Bitcoin has a hard cap of 21 million coins. These are slowly added to the network via the block reward which is currently set to 6.25 bitcoin, roughly every ten minutes.

Halving: Also known as the halvening. This is where the Bitcoin block reward is halved every 210,000 blocks (four years). This reduction in new coins is expected to play a large role in bitcoin's price in the coming years and decades, and is also why the last bitcoin will not be mined for another one hundred years. The current block reward of 6.25 BTC will reduce by 50% to 3.125 BTC in 2024.

Altcoins: This stands for alternative coins. This generally refers to all the cryptocurrencies that came after Bitcoin.

Bitcoin maximalist: This term can be used interchangeably with other coins. For example, you could use the term Ethereum maximalist, although it is generally reserved for Bitcoiners. It describes a person who massively favours one coin and will defend it tooth and nail. Nothing else can compete with their favourite coin. Often you will hear it being used with regards to Bitcoin, as many old school Bitcoin fans have had to defend Bitcoin against the hundreds of newer coins trying to gain some market share or even topple Bitcoin completely.

Market Cap: This is a traditional term from the investing world that is used frequently in cryptocurrency. The market cap of a cryptocurrency is the current price of an individual coin, multiplied by the circulating supply (the amount currently available). It is used as one metric to give an overall figure to a coin's total worth.[32] An important point to note on Market caps: If you study the useful website www.coinmarketcap.com you will notice it lists all the coins in order of their market capitalisation, and not their price. Therefore, you will see some coins valued under £10 in a higher position than some of the more expensive coins. This will be because some coins have hundreds of millions if not billions in circulation, compared to others like Bitcoin and Monero that only have 18 and 17 million respectively. This is an important factor to consider when looking to invest in cryptocurrencies. The position on the above-mentioned website should not be the only pointer in your decision making, lots of due diligence and further education is needed.

FUD: Stands for *Fear, Uncertainty and Doubt*. Some people quite happily spread FUD around the internet on various subjects, including cryptocurrencies. Maybe it's because they don't believe in the particular coin, or its technology, or development team. Or maybe for more nefarious reasons, as unknown to you, they wish to drive the price of the coin down, so they can buy it themselves, cheaper than it was before they started the negative rumour.

FOMO: *Fear of Missing Out*. This term has come from the desire to make the financial gains that some people did in the early days of Bitcoin and some of the other cryptocurrencies. You could argue that most of us have suffered from this feeling from time to time and for varying reasons.

Whales: This is used to describe people who have a lot of cryptocurrency.

---

[32] For example, if bitcoin's price was £12,000 per coin and exactly 19.0 million were in circulation, the total market cap of Bitcoin would be 12,000 x 19,000,000 = £228,000,000,000.

<u>Dust:</u> Dust is very small amounts of cryptocurrency, that are smaller than the average transaction fee. This makes it hard for people to transfer it from their wallet unless they add more funds to the wallet or try to batch different address balances together. Binance allows their members to exchange small amounts of dust in their wallets so that they are not wasted.

<u>DAO:</u> *Decentralised Autonomous Organisation.* This is a business, organisation or product that is managed and controlled by a smart contract (computer code). It is a new concept within the cryptocurrency space and is still in its infancy. A DAO could be designed in such a way that it could self-regulate or manage the funds that it controls. The first-ever DAO was released in April 2016. It was built on the Ethereum blockchain. This DAO was designed to act as a financial fund, that could trade on its own behalf and grow in value over time. A bit like a robotic currency trader. Not long after it went live a hacker found a vulnerability and stole all the ether (Ethereum's native cryptocurrency) inside the DAO, which amounted to hundreds of millions of pounds. This resulted in a hard fork on the Ethereum blockchain to try to recoup the lost ether.

<u>(To the) Moon:</u> This term is used in reference to the price going up (or more accurately the price indicator on the chart rising). The price line on the chart rises at such a steep upwards angle, that it bursts off the top of the chart through the ceiling, out of the roof and up 'to the moon'. On online forums and YouTube videos, you will often hear people asked the question 'When moon'? This became a famous meme and means 'when will the price moon'?

<u>Lambos on the Moon:</u> Lambo refers to the Lamborghini supercar. This phrase most likely evolved from the previous term. Once the price has 'gone to the moon' and the individual has become very wealthy, they then naturally treat themselves to a nice expensive car. So why not make that car a Lamborghini!

<u>Ferraris on Mars</u>: Derived from the previous example, however, it came from an even higher price expectation.

Mars being further away from the earth than the moon, and Ferrari being more desirable than Lamborghini's.

<u>HODL</u>: Stands for *Hold on for Dear Life*. It was a misspelling on an online forum when the individual meant to type the word hold. Hodl is used by the community to mean not to panic sell (if the price drops) and to hold onto their digital asset.
The term is also used in reference to an individual being a long term saver. Aka a 'hodler'. Regardless of the price swings, they are holding for the long term as they believe the cryptocurrency they are hodling (holding) will be worth a great deal more in the future.

<u>Flippening</u>: This is used to describe the switch in dominance from Bitcoin to Ethereum. Bitcoin has always held the number one spot on the website coinmarketcap.com but people are starting to question whether ether will soon take this position away from bitcoin. The two are vastly different, with different use cases and total supplies. However, there seems to be a race on, for some reason, for which will hold the number one spot when listed by its market cap price.

<u>QR Codes</u>: These are the new generation of bar codes. You may have already seen them on packaging, billboards, websites or magazines but never actually used one. You can scan them with an app on your smartphone. Your phone will instantly translate the QR code into something readable or usable, such as loading a website for example. A Bitcoin address (account) can also be represented as a QR code, how cool is that! You can scan a crypto QR code with your wallet on your phone and it will instantly translate it into a Bitcoin receiving address and even insert the address into the *send to* field within your phones Bitcoin wallet. I can foresee a future where high street shops adopt QR codes for cryptocurrency payments.

Next to the checkout till there could be a few different QR codes displayed for the various coins accepted. When you wish to pay with cryptocurrency, you would simply scan the relevant QR code with your phone's cryptocurrency wallet and pay them. The below QR code is my Bitcoin address and if anyone wants to tip me it would be greatly received.

3P4vJM7yVBiPnZh7cDYVqXjxkMFTarb

<u>White Paper</u>: A white paper is a technical paper that a development team publish when they first release their new coin. Most are quite elaborate and difficult to read, as they detail all the science and fundamentals of how their system works. Hardened investors will troll through white papers trying to uncover the projects they deem special. They forearm themselves with this knowledge before others are aware of the coin's specifics, to gain a first movers' advantage.

APPENDIX B

BUYING BITCOIN ON KRAKEN

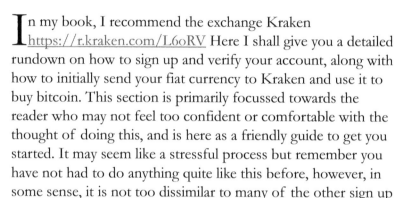

In my book, I recommend the exchange Kraken https://r.kraken.com/L6oRV Here I shall give you a detailed rundown on how to sign up and verify your account, along with how to initially send your fiat currency to Kraken and use it to buy bitcoin. This section is primarily focussed towards the reader who may not feel too confident or comfortable with the thought of doing this, and is here as a friendly guide to get you started. It may seem like a stressful process but remember you have not had to do anything quite like this before, however, in some sense, it is not too dissimilar to many of the other sign up processes you may have already done. Especially if you have a PayPal account that you can fund with your bank account.

I would recommend that you read this whole chapter through first to begin with (or at least each section). Then reread each section carefully, before proceeding with the process at hand to make sure you are clear on what you need to do at each stage.

Shortly I will detail how to buy your first ever bitcoin, but before we do let us look at the topic of price. Also, I should remind the reader that nothing in this book and especially this section is financial or investment advice. In this guide, we are going to complete what is called a *market buy* order. A fancy term, which simply means we are going to buy at the current price. We are not going to do anything special or fancy (having opened an account at Kraken which we shall look at momentarily) we will just jump straight into our account and buy at the price we find bitcoin to be at, the moment we enter the trade page. If you wanted to, you could time your entry and buy bitcoin when it drops a little in price. Or, if you think bitcoin is in a downward trend (meaning it is steadily going down in price) you may want to wait and time your entry accordingly (and get an even better deal). Or maybe bitcoin is in a strong uptrend, where the price is quickly rising hour on hour or day by day. In this case, you *may* wish to not enter now and would rather hold off for a while until the price peaks and possibly retraces a little.

All this may sound complicated, but over time and with a little experience, (and especially if you wish to learn) it may become second nature to you and you could become skilled at timing your entries a little more carefully. However, people don't need to learn this skill. Earlier in this book, I briefly mentioned a system called dollar-cost averaging (DCA). This is where you do not try to time your entry and just buy at set times, whether that is weekly or monthly, such as after every payday for example.[33] Some people do not believe DCA works. I personally believe most beginners *do* use the DCA system. Your only other option is to watch the price and enter when *you* think you are getting the best deal. There is lots of information on the internet on how to time this, and the topic falls heavily under a method called Technical Analysis (TA).[34] Either way, regardless of the techniques you use, it is up to the reader to decide how and at what price point they intend to enter a buy order. Whether you

---

[33] You buy regardless of the bitcoin price and because you buy systematically, sometimes you buy when the price is a little high and other times you buy when the price is a little low. Because of these differences, over time, the overall average of your position is flattened out, meaning overall you pay a more average price.

[34] Among other things, TA shows you how to 'read' the price charts along with the candlesticks and patterns within them. Search the internet or YouTube for 'bitcoin TA' and you will find lots of information on this. Please note, that although hundreds of thousands of traders (traditional and crypto) use TA daily, some people do not believe it works or that it can help in trading. Traders who use TA will strongly refute this point and say without TA they would not make their large gains.

wait for an opportune moment or utilise the DCA system and buy regardless of the price, nothing I have summarised here is investment or trading advice. The steps we will take in a few moments will be to buy bitcoin at the current price (unless you personally hold off buying until the price reaches one you are happier with). The only risk in waiting, is obviously that the price may rise and then you ultimately lose out and end up having to pay more...herein the conundrum. Let's now look at the items needed and the process of joining Kraken and the exciting step of entering the new economy.

Items needed

- PC with an internet connection.

- One form of government ID such as a driver's licence, passport or national ID card that is valid and has not expired.

- One proof of residence such as a utility bill, credit card, bank or insurance statement, which was issued within the last 3 months. If you don't have any of these pieces of information follow my referral link https://r.kraken.com/L6oRV and search for the list of items you can use.

- Email address (preferably a new one).

- A password that you have created specifically to use on Kraken (preferably one that is at least 12 characters long). Ideally, this should be a random-looking string of characters such as K89&g53$@kDfjhH5. (Please don't copy my suggestion. Make yours unique and store it safely).

Preparation

- Before you start you will want to have a couple of things ready and already stored on your computer. This will be a scan or photo of your government-issued identification, and your proof of residence.

- When you scan or photo these items, be sure they are in colour. Also, make sure that the whole card/document is included and that it takes up most of the image space, and that this is done in good lighting conditions. If you do not make the image as clear as possible, Kraken may reject the image and ask that you resubmit it to them. Make sure the proof of residence document includes your address and is no older than 3 months and that your ID has not expired. If for any reason you do not fulfil Kraken's criteria, you may be asked to also submit an IDCP (Identity Confirmation Photo) which is a photo of yourself holding a piece of paper with your signature, the day's date and the words kraken.com written on it. It is an additional security check which will be required if the information you initially provided was incorrect or invalid for any reason. This does seem like an odd request, but it is something that other exchanges also ask for in certain circumstances.

- One other thing a reader may wish to do (as I detailed in the security chapter) is to make a brand new email address. This will (hopefully) shield you to some extent and if nothing else, means that only correspondence with Kraken will go to this new email address, so that should your normal email address become compromised (because you use it in so many different places), this will not put your Kraken account at any possible risk. This step is not essential, but one that many Bitcoiners would recommend as being sensible. The choice is yours, a new email address will only take a couple of minutes to create.

My advice would be to not include your name or other personal details in this new email address.

<u>Signing up for a Kraken account</u>

- Now that you have your ID scans/photos stored on your PC (and hopefully a new email address) you can follow my referral link here <u>https://r.kraken.com/L6oRV</u> and we can get you signed up. On Kraken's sign up page, you will need to add your new email, a username and a password. Your username does *not* have to be your real name (again more security to protect your identity, wherever possible). Remember your Kraken password should not be one you use elsewhere, and it should also be very strong. Note: Make sure you write down your username and password and keep them safe. Having added this information and then clicking the proceed button you will be redirected to an activation page.

- Kraken will email you a special code called an Activation Key, that will be needed on this activation page. You will also need to retype your Kraken password and username, so be sure to have made a note of them.

- Now your account is activated you can log in and view your brand new Kraken account. Well done you! Next, you will need to decide what service you require. Kraken offers three different account types. As you are wanting to be able to transfer your fiat currency from your bank account to Kraken, you will need to choose the *Intermediate* account. Click on your account button which is located on the top right of the page (the circular button) and click on Verify Account. You will be redirected to a new page where you will need to insert your name, date of birth, address etc.

Make sure the information you enter here is all correct, as failure to add correct info will breach Krakens terms and conditions. All the information you add will be stored safely by Kraken and is ultimately needed for Kraken to comply with the KYC (Know Your Customer) banking legislation we mentioned earlier in the book. Clicking to continue takes you to yet another page, where you will now need to upload your scans/photos of your government ID and proof of residence that you saved to your PC earlier.

- Once you have uploaded your ID and submitted this information, your verification status will shift to pending. Meaning Kraken's system will be working to validate the information you have given them. Depending on the demands being put on their system this may take a couple of days, however, in many cases this will only take a few hours. If by the second day nothing appears to have happened and you have not received a confirmation email you should contact Kraken support via their website. Keep an eye on your emails to see if they are trying to contact you (this includes your Spam/Junk folder as their emails might accidentally go there). Once you have a verified account you are a full member of Kraken. All that is left for you to do is send some fiat currency to your Kraken account and to finally buy your first bitcoin.

<u>Funding your Kraken account</u>

- To add funds to your Kraken account we need to navigate to the Funding page, by following the fund button on the top of the main home page. Here you can see your account balances. To start the process of adding funds to your Kraken account, look for your fiat currency of choice on the list provided. In the UK we use Pound Sterling also known as Great British Pound (GBP). There are also other options here such as the US Dollar and the Euro. To the right of your currency, you can see the deposit and withdraw buttons in blue. Click on the deposit button.

- Now you are given the option to select a deposit method. I recommend selecting the option: **Clear Junction (FPS/BACS)**. Clear Junction is the name of Krakens bank. FPS is the Faster Payment Service and BACS is another bank payment service. Feel free to research the other two options, however for most people (unless you are looking to deposit very large sums of fiat currency they will not be suitable. For example, the CHAPS option may be faster but will cost you much more.

- Once you click on Clear Junction FPS/BACS you will see all the information needed to send your fiat currency to Kraken, via their bank account (Clear Junction). **Carefully read the information that appears, such as how important it is that you include the reference code provided**. As this shows both Clear Junction and Kraken, which account you are trying to fund (that being *your* Kraken account). Also, note that this deposit must come from your bank account and that you cannot use a third party such as a friend or family member to pay fiat into your Kraken account. It *must* come from an account, whose name matches the name on your Kraken account. **Only you can fund your Kraken account!**

- Here you will also see there is a small fee to send this deposit. Kraken is charged by their bank so unfortunately they pass this charge onto us. This cannot be helped and is a small price to pay for entering the new economy. Most exchanges will charge a fee for this, along with another small fee at the point of actually buying the cryptocurrency. These fees vary from exchange to exchange and Kraken is one of the cheaper options available. Most financial products and investments incur a fee at the point of purchase and are referred in many cases as the premium. When investors buy gold or silver, for example, there is a small premium added to the spot price at the point of purchase. When buying shares there is also a fee that the broker charges. If we remind ourselves that these fees are needed to enter the new economy we can forgo being too upset by this. Besides, we hope that the bitcoin we are soon to purchase will rise in value and we can recoup these fees. (Not investment advice. Please remember that bitcoin's price may drop immediately after you buy. Your capital is at risk in all financial markets, including the new crypto market).

- Now that you have settled on the payment method and are aware of the information/terms presented, you can proceed with funding your Kraken account. This means you need to open another page within your browser (or your phones banking app) and navigate to and log into your online bank account. If you do not bank online, it may be a good time to learn how to and set yourself up to do so. You could see banking online as the first training steps to preparing yourself to enter the crypto world. If online banking is too much to handle but you do want to fund your Kraken account, you will need to pop into your bank branch or phone them to relay the payment information. For most people, where online banking is an option you will just need to create a payment to a new recipient within your online account. At the time of writing, the account name/Payee we need to pay is: Payward Ltd. We obviously need to add the supplied sort code and account number and be sure to add the 16 character reference number that Kraken provides so that your deposit goes to your Kraken account.

- Once the payment has gone through from your bank you will just have to wait a short while until it is received by Kraken and has been deposited into your Kraken account. They will email you a confirmation once this has been completed. This process usually takes less than an hour to complete and in many cases is done within ten or so minutes.

Buying your first bitcoin: Introduction

Well, here we are. The final step. All these hours of reading my book. All this learning and preparation, all boiled down to this one moment in time. It may even turn into a famous story that you tell your children or grandchildren.

Before we continue let's just cover a couple of points. Throughout my whole book, we have referred to bitcoin as BTC. In recent months there has been a push by some of the larger exchanges to change the ticker symbol to XBT.[35] At Kraken, they have already made the move, so within your account you will notice that they refer to bitcoin as XBT.

It is important to note that although this process may seem stressful to begin with, like many other things we do, it will become *much* easier with repetition. Take your online banking for example. To begin with, you may have felt quite nervous using it, however, it is possible that you now whizz around your online bank account, clicking here and there, almost on autopilot. (Having said that, it is important to take your time when buying, sending or trading cryptocurrency and I do not

---

[35] This is to keep in line with the traditional exchange market standards and shows that Bitcoin is gaining some street cred and legitimacy as an international currency. The standard dictates that if a currency is not associated with a particular country it should start with an X.

want to give you the impression you should merrily click around willy-nilly), only that in time your confidence will grow. Remember that earlier in the book we learnt that crypto is a push network, where you are in total control of your addresses and once you push crypto from your wallet, there is generally nothing that *anyone* can do to assist you should you have made a mistake in the process. Now that you have joined Kraken you are in good hands, but even so, you really want to be cautious and methodical with your actions, as even Kraken will not be able to help you with lost bitcoin.

So back to the monumental moment at hand. You have a Kraken account. There is fiat currency inside your account, waiting to be swapped for its more glamourous crypto cousin, bitcoin. Let's quickly review the steps we will take before jumping in. Please remember to read through each section first, before going ahead with any of the actions required, to be sure you have a good understanding of what we are about to do. It's going to be relatively simple, so you don't need to be too scared. This is meant to be the fun bit, the point where you join the new economy.

The overview

- Once you have completed all the steps above, we are ready to buy bitcoin.

- We will navigate to the trade page.

- We will select buying XBT with GBP (buying bitcoin with pounds). If you're not using pounds select your national currency.

- We will select the amount of bitcoin we want to buy.

- We will hit the buy button.

Buying your first bitcoin

Let's get this party started and buy your first bitcoin. Remember that here, we are going to buy at the current price and not do anything fancy like time our entry for a specific price. It will be up to the reader to learn how to do that by themselves. Here we are going to enter a *market buy order* and buy bitcoin at the current price.

- On the Kraken home page, click the Trade button located in the top menu.

- On the trade page, you will see that some useful information is located within the dark blue stripe near the top of the page. Inside this stripe is a silver tab on the left and a few different words and figures. I will quickly detail what a couple of these mean to give you a better understanding of what is being displayed here. Firstly, on the left inside the dark stripe, you will see a silver tab with XBT/GBP. This is the trading pair we are currently selected on, as we want to buy bitcoin with pounds. If you are using a different fiat currency to buy your bitcoin please select accordingly. Once you have experience with Kraken's system and if you wish to branch out into the other cryptocurrencies they offer, you can select that tab and browse the other coins they have. For the moment though, let's leave it as it is (XBT/GBP) and continue now looking in that dark blue stripe at the top of the page. Next to the silver tab, you should be able to see the word LAST, with a figure next to it. This is the most recent price of bitcoin (XBT/BTC) in pounds, the latest or last price. This figure will change continually, as the price of bitcoin is always moving. The next figure to the right is the HIGH. This is the highest price bitcoin has hit today. Further to the right, we have the word LOW.

This is the lowest price bitcoin has hit over the same period. These three figures will help you in your price analysis and may help you in deciding if the Last price (the current price) is a good deal or not. As we are planning to execute a market buy and plan to buy our bitcoin straight away, regardless of the price, we don't need to bother ourselves with any price analysis. However, it is nice to see what the current price is, along with today's high and low prices.

- On the left-hand side and just under the above-mentioned XBT/GBP silver tab, you will notice a tab highlighted in blue called New Order. Underneath this tab you will see a smaller blue highlighted tab, showing we are on a Simple order screen. Next to simple, are the unhighlighted words, intermediate and advanced. Let's keep things simple for now and stay on the Simple, New Order page. Later, once you have more experience you may wish to check out the other order pages.

- A little below the blue highlighted Simple tab, on the left-hand side, we can see a green buy tab. We want to make sure the tab is highlighted green. (If the sell tab is highlighted it turns red).

- Now look to the right of the green buy tab. Let's briefly get accustomed to what we are seeing. We have an empty box with the amount of bitcoin (XBT/BTC) we wish to buy. To the right of this, we have an empty box with the amount of GBP we wish to spend. To the right of this, we have a tab with the words, MARKET/LIMIT. Then next to this we have an estimated total of GBP we are going to spend. These boxes allow us to set the parameters of the order we wish to place.

- As we are going to complete a *market buy* order, we need to select the **MARKET** tab and not the Limit tab. Under the price box, you will see the sentence 'Buy XBT at the best market price'. (When you have gained some experience, you may wish to use the Limit tab. Using a limit buy order, you will be able to select the price you wish to pay. Kraken will then open your order, but it will not execute your order until your specified price has been reached).

- Today, however (with your consent and understanding), we are going to buy right now. So, select the Market tab and then type into the XBT box, the amount of bitcoin you wish to buy. Note: If you hover your mouse over the price box, you will see a red no entry sign appear. This is because you can't adjust the XBT price you are wanting to buy at, because we are buying at the market price. (If you select the Limit tab, then you *could* adjust the price accordingly).

- With the Market tab highlighted, as you type in the amount of XBT you wish to buy, you will see the box on the far right, fill with the estimated cost of the purchase. Obviously, you want to make sure the amount this order will cost, is equal to or less than the total amount of GBP you have in your account. Adjust the amount of XBT accordingly until you are happy with the amount of bitcoin you are going to buy and the amount it will cost you in pounds (or your fiat currency of choice).

- We are just about ready to take your first step into the new economy. You have filled in all the required boxes. We have a simple, buy order page open. We have selected the green buy bitcoin (XBT) tab. You have selected the amount of XBT you wish to buy, and are happy with the estimated total figure on the far right, and are happy it is equal to or less than the total amount of fiat you have in your Kraken account. All that is left to do is click the large green buy XBT with GBP button. I would recommend leaving that small box next to the buy button, unchecked and allow for order confirmations to continue. If nothing else, continue with confirmations until you become comfortable and familiar with the buying and selling process.

(This is not in relation to bitcoin confirmations that we learnt about in the book, just a simple Kraken confirmation that all the details you have entered are correct).

- When you click the large green buy button, Kraken will then take you to a confirmation page, where you will need to quickly check all the details.

- If you are happy with everything you have entered on the buy page - Click that green buy button and buy your first bitcoin! There you have it, congratulations! If you care to look at the top right of the page, you will see your account overview and notice that your account balance has changed. Your fiat balance has reduced and your XBT balance now records your first bitcoin purchase!

- If you navigate to the orders page by hitting the orders tab, you will see the order you have just executed is included in the closed orders section, as it was instantly completed by Kraken and it is now closed. If in the future, should you open a limit order (as you wanted to enter a limit buy order at a particular price) you would now see your open limit order in the open order section, as it is unlikely that your limit order has been immediately fulfilled, as the price you set may not have been reached just yet. You will have to be patient and wait. If the price moves against you, you can still wait, or you can cancel the order (if you wish) and set a new limit order, or you could simply set a market order (like we have just done) and buy at the current price. In which case you can click on the New Order tab.

- The only thing left for me to mention is that when you log into Kraken you will likely see a reminder to secure your account with 2FA (two-factor authentication) such as the Google Authenticator app or a YubiKey.

Both were mentioned in the book and I strongly recommend you consider using one of these systems to protect your Kraken account. The Google app is free, while a YubiKey costs around £45. I would only recommend the YubiKey to people who are striving for an extra level of security, beyond that of just the Google app itself. Both the YubiKey and Google Authenticator app can be used on many sites to help you protect them. You may wish to reread the security chapter in this book, where the Google app is discussed and remember to make a backup of the recovery password Kraken provide you at the point you protect your account with 2FA. Kraken will do their best to protect your account and your bitcoin, however, it is also your responsibility to endeavour to protect yourself. Search YouTube or the internet and learn all you can about these two systems.

Congratulations are in order. You have now made the leap and entered the new economy. You are the proud owner of some bitcoin. You should be quite proud of yourself and definitely pop the kettle on and make yourself a nice cup of tea or pour that cocktail. You are now a member of the crypto world and can hold your head up high. If for whatever reason something went wrong during your attempt to buy bitcoin, you can contact Kraken support who will happily set you back on track. Now that you hold your bitcoin on Kraken you must consider where you wish to keep it in the long term. As we learnt in the book, holding small amounts on Kraken is not an issue, but ideally, we need to get you up and running with your own wallet so you can take complete custody/control of your private keys for yourself. For those who want to jump straight into self-custody, please visit https://www.thebitcoinbook.co.uk and look at my videos and links. With a Nano X you will be able to send your new bitcoin from Kraken to your hardware wallet and store them safely all by yourself. Alternatively, if you do not want to purchase a hardware wallet you could look at downloading a PC wallet (see Wallet Software in the index). That's enough excitement for one day and once again congratulations on joining the new economy.

APPENDIX C

HARDWARE WALLET SECURITY

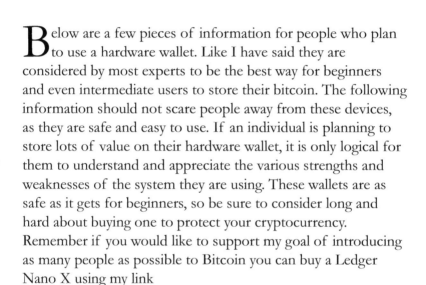

B elow are a few pieces of information for people who plan to use a hardware wallet. Like I have said they are considered by most experts to be the best way for beginners and even intermediate users to store their bitcoin. The following information should not scare people away from these devices, as they are safe and easy to use. If an individual is planning to store lots of value on their hardware wallet, it is only logical for them to understand and appreciate the various strengths and weaknesses of the system they are using. These wallets are as safe as it gets for beginners, so be sure to consider long and hard about buying one to protect your cryptocurrency. Remember if you would like to support my goal of introducing as many people as possible to Bitcoin you can buy a Ledger Nano X using my link https://www.ledger.com?r=e965d9125b6e The Nano X allows people to safely store up to 100 different cryptocurrencies at the same time.

- Initialise (set up) these hardware wallets at home on your own internet connection. Do this slowly and calmly being sure to follow the instructions the manufacturer provides you. Do not rush this process and do not initialise these devices on a shared public internet connection.

- When using these devices, trust the information you are presented with on the screen of the hardware wallet itself, and not what you see on your computer or phone's screen. Your PC or phone could be compromised whereas your hardware wallet is secure and should be trusted over your internet device.

- As safe as these hardware devices are, there are some security practices that we should adhere to. Your hardware wallet should be kept safe and not be allowed to fall into the hands of a hacker/thief, as some models are susceptible to physical attack, where the individual who has gained possession of the device can ultimately steal the bitcoin the device is protecting. This can even be done without having the 4-8 digit pin that we use to unlock the device. To clarify, these devices are extremely secure while being used over the internet, *this* advice relates to a thief gaining physical access to the hardware wallet. For this reason, do not leave your hardware wallet lying around, it should be stored either out of sight or even secured away in a safe. Note: Your average criminal will not be able to retrieve any bitcoin from your device, as it takes in-depth knowledge and also a machine which costs hundreds of thousands of pounds and uses a laser to attack the hardware wallet! Should you believe your device has been compromised in any way, or you discover it has been stolen, my advice would be to quickly download a PC/phone wallet and restore access to your bitcoin quickly on this new wallet using the restore wallet function and your seed phrase.[36] Then having regained access, you should quickly move the bitcoin to a totally new wallet **(which importantly has a new 12-24 word seed phrase)**.

In doing so you will now have emptied your original wallet, so any attacker (who does have the ability to hack into the

---

[36] Some people purchase a second hardware wallet and have it ready in reserve, so that should the first one break or get stolen they have a second one ready at hand and can quickly restore their wallet on the spare device. This is obviously not a necessity and is just a clever step in being extra prepared should something happen to your original hardware wallet.

device) now only has access to an 'empty' hardware wallet and its empty addresses. Your bitcoin is now safely stored in a brand new wallet, which again has a totally new seed phrase.

- Another good security practice is not to buy second-hand hardware wallets, as you do not know what the seller may have done to the internals, as they may have compromised the security of the device. Only buy directly from the manufacturer or licenced resellers. Following my link will take you directly to the company Ledger and allow you to purchase the Ledger Nano X directly from them.

- If when you receive your wallet in the post, it looks like the packaging has been tampered with in any way, do not use it and contact the manufacturer.

- Most manufacturers supply you with a small piece of card to write your seed phrase on to when you initialise your device for the first time. One scam out there is receiving your hardware wallet with the recovery phrase sheet already pre-filled with words. In this scam, a person has somehow intercepted your delivery, (or maybe you've tried to save yourself a few pounds and have bought a second-hand wallet instead of going directly to the manufacturer). When you receive the hardware wallet, the blank recovery seed phrase sheet has already been filled in. This has been done to make you think that this is your 'factory supplied seed phrase'. This will *never* be the case; the card should always be blank when you receive it, as your new wallet will generate your seed phrase for you when you turn it on for the first time.

- Another tip is to add an additional layer of security to your device by adding a passphrase to your wallet. This is something I cannot easily detail as executing this will vary depending on the device you own, so search for the manufacturer's instructions on how to complete this security upgrade. This option is only recommended for intermediate to advanced users.

- The *Stephan Livera Podcast* has aired a series on hardware wallets, which I strongly recommend anyone who has (or is planning to) put lots of fiat currency into this market should listen to. SLP96 features Max Hillebrand and SLP97 Michael Flaxman, both of which are good episodes and will show you that these hardware wallets are extremely safe for beginners and even intermediate users but, for the more advanced user and investors with *extremely* deep pockets, more facts should be learnt. They predominately cover the points I have raised in this section, but all the same it is sometimes best to hear advice directly from the professionals. All these episodes are available on YouTube along with most good podcast applications.

Please remember that it is not my aim to scare anyone away from Bitcoin, but to show you how to best protect yourself and to detail all possible security risks. Most of the threats I have detailed in this book will not be experienced by 99% of my readers, but it only seemed right that I mention them so that everyone is at least aware of the possible threats. One final podcast/YouTube episode for people who wish to learn more on security is from the *What Bitcoin Did* channel. The host, Peter McCormack has released a beginner series on everything Bitcoin. In episode #12 he interviews Jameson Lopp, a privacy focussed advanced bitcoin user and entrepreneur. In this episode, you will learn many ways you can increase your Op-Sec (operational security) both in general internet life and from 34 minutes into the interview the chat focusses on Bitcoin security.

ABOUT THE AUTHOR

Matthew Underhill is an author and entrepreneur with over 5 years of experience with Cryptocurrency. He has been fascinated with Bitcoin and the potential it has to transform finance ever since first discovering the technology in 2014. Now, he hopes to share what he's learnt with his readers, teaching them the wonders of Bitcoin and how to make the most of this cryptocurrency revolution. He lives in the South West of England with his wife, young daughter and their dogs. While not working and looking after his young family, Matt can be found tinkering on his campervan, clay pigeon shooting and playing rugby. To reach out to Matt, or to find all the products and services he recommends, please visit his website. https://www.thebitcoinbook.co.uk

INDEX

A

address.....76, 78, 81, 82, 83, 89, 90, 93, 94, 95, 96, 169, 247, 252, 264
adoption 44, 45, 56, 159, 160, 161, 209, 211, 212
Adoption Bell Curve 161
alphanumeric 93
Amous, Saifedean65, 66, 68, 69, 71, 108, 122, 241, 245
anarchist 23, 25
Antonopoulos, Andreas M. 108, 157, 159, 241, 242, 243, 245
ASIC 112, 113
Austrian 24, 25, 65, 66

B

Baby Boomers 58
Back, Adam................. 22, 73
backup 89, 90, 92, 97, 98, 101, 194, 203, 233
Bank of England 8
Binance ..106, 144, 163, 165, 166, 167, 180, 204, 214, 251
Binance token (BNB) 180
Bitcoin
money/unit of account (little b) 34, 41, 47, 51, 55,

56, 57, 68, 71, 76, 78, 81, 83, 84, 90, 107, 108, 111, 217, 226, 236
technology (big B) 30, 34, 35, 36, 48, 51, 76, 77, 78, 81, 83, 111, 209, 229, 233, 234
Bitcoin Cash (BCH) 139
Bitcoin Satoshi's Vision (BSV)...............................144
BitGold 21, 22
block reward. 108, 110, 111, 112, 114, 147, 182, 226
block size 139, 140, 142
blockchain..... 36, 37, 48, 76, 78, 81, 83, 84, 85, 100, 102, 109, 110, 111, 118, 119, 129, 139, 143, 174, 211
blockchain analysis 32
blocks 83, 110, 111, 119, 120, 122, 139, 140, 148, 205
B-money............................22
brain drain 160
Bretton Woods agreement8, 14
bull market................ 53, 236
burning............................181
Byzantine General's Problem..........................117

C

Cantillon Effect............... 10
Capsule .... *See* Cryptosteel
censorship-resistant ..37, 48, 132, 247
central bank..... 8, 11, 14, 20, 66, 70, 230
Chaum, David 22
CoinJoin 153
coinmarketcap 53, 250
cold storage. *See* wallets (hot & cold)
Coldcard 105
commodity 4, 5, 7, 8, 27, 42, 55, 56, 61, 63, 67, 71, 152, 226
confirmations.. 76, 119, 120, 121, 126, 220
consensus 114, 115, 117, 118
crypto-anarchists 23
cryptography. 22, 25, 32, 36, 37, 38, 77, 78, 151
Cryptosteel 99, 106, 167, 195, 203
custodian 91, 100, 219
cypherpunk ... 22, 23, 38, 73, 221

D

Dai, Wei........................... 22
DAO 251
DApp 174, 178, 181, 244

DCA .... *See* dollar -cost averaging
decentralised.....31, 166, 177
decryption 77
devaluation 5, 246
DEX 163, 166, 167
difficulty adjustment..... 109, 110, 112, 113, 150
digital gold 35, 55, 178
divisible 41, 42, 61, 66
dollar-cost averaging 227, 256, 257

E

Ecash 22
economist (also see Austrian/Keynesian) 24, 25, 65, 245
encryption 77, 99
Enigma 77, 151
entrepreneurs 15, 25, 72, 220, 248
EOS 133, 164, 179, 180, 186, 187
ERC20.................... 177, 186
ether.........................132, 133
Ethereum 132, 148, 177, 178, 183, 186
Everything Bubble....*See* The Everything Bubble

F

FCA 171
Federal Reserve..8, 235, 246

fiat currency 9
file 38, 83, 90, 91
Financial Conduct
Authority .... *See* FCA
Finney, Hal 21, 22, 27
fleecing .... *See* haircut
fork 129, 139, 141, 142, 144,
145, 149, 154, 180, 251
fractional reserve banking 11
Friedman, Milton 25
fungible 66, 153

G

Gen X 57, 58
Gen Z 71
global reserve currency 7,
12, 14
Gold
gold sovereign 4, 5
gold standard 65
Gold Standard 7, 8, 9, 69, 70
World Gold Council 57
Google Authenticator .. 197,
268
Great Recession (2008) .. 10,
13, 14, 229, 231

H

hackers 94, 98, 101, 103,
193, 200
haircut 58
Hanyecz, Laszlo 43, 122
hash 248
hash rate 110

Hashcash 22
hashing power 109, 137
HMRC 152, 211
hodler 224, 252
hyperinflation ... 10, 160, 246

I

ICO. *See* initial coin offering
immutable 48, 86, 110
inflation 5, 12, 17, 52, 57, 58
initial coin offering 171, 172,
179, 182, 183, 185, 187, 189
input 85
IOTA 122, 148, 183
IRS 152, 211

K

Keepkey 105
Keynesian 25, 65, 230
keys 89, 90, 91, 92, 93, 96,
97, 100, 101, 102, 103, 106,
168, 219
private key 89, 90, 91, 92,
93, 96, 98, 100, 101, 102,
103, 169, 201, 202
public key 89, 90
Kraken ... 106, 163, 167, 217,
255, 259

L

Ledger (hardware wallet)
.... 102, 103, 105, 106, 167,
199, 214, 269, 271, 273

ledger (technology) ..81, 241
Lee, Charlie 179
leveraged trading ...223, 224, 234
libertarian 23
Lightning Network 121, 122, 125, 126, 127, 241
Livera, Stephan 227, 241, 242, 243, 274
LN ...See Lightning Network
Lopp, Jameson 241, 243, 274

M

MaidSafeCoin (MAID) . 136
McCormack, Peter 241, 242, 274
mempool 119
Menger, Carl 25
micropayments 121, 122
middleman ....See third party
Millennials 57, 58, 71
Mining
centralisation................... 139
cloud 107
contract........................... 114
difficulty ....See difficulty adjustment
farms 111, 149
gold 57, 67
mining bitcoin..... 21, 68, 76, 107, 108, 111, 112, 113, 150, 155, 157
pool mining.................... 109

power..See hashing power & hash rate
pre-mining 183
solo mining..................... 109
Mises Institute............ 24, 25
Mises, Ludwig Von...........25
mixing services See CoinJoin
Monero (XMR) 149, 163, 164, 181, 250
Money
government money 5, 9
hard money... 66, 68, 69, 71, 121, 230, 245
monopoly (paper money)..8
old money 1, 2, 4
sound money.....1, 9, 65, 66, 236
Mt. Gox.......................... 168
multisig..... 94, 169, 201, 202

N

Nakamoto .... See Satoshi
Nano X ....See Ledger (hardware wallet)
nanopayments 121, 122
Nixon shock' 8
node ...36, 81, 139, 142, 219, 220, 248
Non-Fungible Token 174

O

open source 29, 86, 131
operational security . 93, 274
output 85

P

pandemic 5, 14, 229
password .. 90, 195, 197, 204
password manager . 196, 203
Paul, Ron 17, 25
permissionless 38
pizza 43, 122, 144
Plan B 227, 241, 242
PoS .... *See* proof-of-stake
PoW .... *See* proof-of-work
printing .... *See* quantitative easing
privacy 22, 95, 136, 149, 153, 172, 181, 203, 221, 274
privacy coins .. 149, 172, 181
private key .... *See* keys
proof-of-stake 108, 114, 115, 183, 187
proof-of-work 107, 108, 112, 114, 115, 183, 187
public key .... *See* keys
purchasing power 5, 52, 229, 233, 235

Q

QR code 93, 239, 252
QuadrigaCX 169
quantitative easing. 5, 10, 13, 14, 65, 230
Quintillion 95, 110

R

Rai stones 2, 130

random .. 89, 95, 96, 97, 112, 196
restore wallet ... 99, 100, 102, 272
Rothbard, Murray 25
RPOW 22

S

S2F .... *See* stock-to-flow
Satoshi
person 20, 21, 22, 29, 34, 235
unit 41, 42, 126, 148, 236
Sats (s) .... *See* Satoshi (unit)
scytale 77
SEC 171, 188
Secure Hash Algorithm .. *See* SHA-256
Securities Exchange Commission .... *See* SEC
security 94, 105, 169, 189, 192, 197, 201, 202, 235, 243, 272, 273, 274
security token offering .. 174, 189, 190
seed phrase 97, 98, 100, 102, 167, 194, 204, 233, 273
SegWit 142
SHA-256 21
silk road 23
SIM swapping 197, 198
smart contract 132, 133, 136, 178, 179, 181, 183, 205, 211, 251

spot trading................224
Stablecoin......172, 187, 205, 214
Stellar (XLM).164, 180, 181
STO..........*See* security token offering
stock market 10, 13, 71, 229
stock-to-flow..... 67, 68, 228
store of value.... 17, 71, 121, 132, 154, 172
Szabo, Nick................21, 22

T

TA....*See* Technical Analysis
Technical Analysis .227, 256
The Everything Bubble.. 13, 14, 230
The World Bank............ 159
third party.....35, 37, 38, 118
time preference...........62, 69
token.......................171, 173
tokenisation.................... 189
transaction..... 19, 20, 37, 81, 86, 107, 119, 139, 140, 142, 148, 154, 169, 220
transaction fee .. 86, 87, 109, 112, 140, 141, 251
Trezor............................ 105
Tron (TRX)... 133, 164, 181, 182, 186
trustless.......................... 118
tulip bulbs.......................... 2
two-factor authentication 196, 197, 200, 204, 268

U

Unspent Transaction Output................ *See* UTXO
UTXO..............................85

V

value........1, 4, 8, 47, 48, 108
VeChain (VET)..... 122, 135, 163
Venezuela.................. 10, 160
Virtual Private Network .*See* VPN
volatility.......... 173, 225, 226
Voorhees, Erik......... 34, 241
VPN.............................. 203

W

Wallet..............................97
brain wallets.................... 102
exchange wallets 105
hardware wallets............. 103
hierarchical deterministic (HD) 97, 105, 192
hot & cold wallets.101, 102, 103, 105
paper wallets................... 102
PC and phone wallets ... 102
restore....... *See* restore wallet
Wallet Software
Abra................................ 103
Atomic Wallet 103
Coinomi 103
Edge................................ 103

Green wallet.................... 103
Ledger *See* Ledger (hardware wallet)
wallet words *See* seed phrase
Weimar Republic.............. 10
white paper 253

Y

YubiKey.................. 197, 268

Z

Zimbabwe........................10
Zuck-Bucks 206

Printed in Great Britain
by Amazon